"This deeply touching and beautifully written book shows us how to bring acceptance and tender support to every part of ourselves, for healing and happiness and love. Grounded in science, endlessly practical and effective, and full of inspiring stories, it's a gem."

RICK HANSON, PhD, *New York Times*–bestselling author, *Resilient* and *Hardwiring Happiness*

"With keen insight, compassion, and disarming honesty, Dr. Parker has distilled her deep wisdom born of years of clinical practice and personal investigation into a step-by-step guide to authentically connecting with ourselves. This book can help almost anyone live a richer, more engaged, more empowered life by tapping our inner healing potential while boldly facing the enormous challenges of being human."

DR. RONALD D. SIEGEL, assistant professor of psychology, Harvard Medical School; author, *The Extraordinary Gift of Being Ordinary*

"From page one, I was in love with *Embracing Unrest* and highlighting the heck out of Sandra's insights. As someone who believes the body is the way to real change and lasting insight, I can't recommend this book highly enough. I believe this book has the power to change your life and our hurting world."

JENNIFER LOUDEN, national bestselling author, *The Woman's Comfort Book* and *Why Bother?*

"The rest we seek can only be found if we turn around to head into the very feelings we have been running away from. A frightening thought to be sure, but Dr. Parker eases our alarm with a generous invitation to embrace our most vulnerable selves, heart-warming stories to illustrate the journey, and practical suggestions to guide our way. Many thanks to Sandra for this much-needed assurance and encouragement that embracing our vulnerability is indeed worth it!"

DR. GORDON NEUFELD, bestselling author (with Dr. Gabor Maté), *Hold Onto Your Kids*; founder, the Neufeld Institute

"If only everyone would read this book! Dr. Parker's richly informed and beautiful writing voice inspires us to ride the roller coaster of life by leaning into its terrifying turns, dips, and upward climbs while trusting the full range of our feelings to take us safely home. She courageously shares her darkest hours and has lived what she teaches. Dr. Parker implores us to embrace unrest by tuning in to the most crucial resources of our lifetime, our bodily signals and emotions. She beckons us with compassion and tenderness toward a profoundly nourishing relationship with ourselves."

SUSAN WARREN WARSHOW, LCSW, founder, DEFT Institute; author, *A Therapist's Handbook to Dissolve Shame and Defense*

"The mind and body are intimately linked for health and well-being, and this powerful book introduces a very subtle yet extremely important inner signal to help us tune in to ourselves. Embracing unrest is the ultimate self-regulation practice that holds the key to sustainable mental and physical health. Dr. Parker skillfully navigates her readers to explore emotions and experience and what it means to be fully present in our daily lives."

DR. BAL PAWA, physician; bestselling author, *The Mind-Body Cure*

"Unrest points to the wisdom within ourselves that we have not yet listened to. But how do we do that? We need to listen to our vulnerability with the ear of the heart. With great gentleness, Dr. Parker invites us to use the physical experience of unrest as a cue to pay inner attention to soothe the body and harness emotion. If we can slow down, tune in to, and listen to our bodies, we can receive the information the mind does not yet have. If you've wondered how to tune in to your feelings to find the relief you seek, this book offers powerful guidance to help you feel deeply and live fully."

JON FREDERICKSON, bestselling author, *The Lies We Tell Ourselves, Create a Better Life, Co-Creating Change,* and *Co-Creating Safety*

"*Embracing Unrest* is a fresh and excellent exploration of turning toward what is most difficult, scary, painful, to-be-avoided-at-all-costs as the most reliable path toward being fully alive and whole. Dr. Parker is a knowledgeable and trustworthy guide to listening deeply and patiently to our innermost vulnerabilities—little moments of unrest—that can reliably lead to big choices and genuine transformations. We recognize ourselves in the many stories of real people, struggling as we do, learning to work with unrest as our most powerful ally in healing and growth. The science is solid and sensible. The practices are embodied, doable exercises to change your way of being with yourself (WIN—warmth, interest, nonjudgment) that become the doorway to deeper authenticity, resilience, and connection. The journey itself is the gift."

LINDA GRAHAM, MFT, bestselling author, *Bouncing Back*

"This beautiful book invites you to listen to the wisdom of your body as it calls you home to feel the truth and grow in the most important moments of your life, when your longing meets your limits. *Embracing Unrest* shows you how to do the opposite of how you are wired and approach the discomfort of vulnerability so you can live your most powerfully authentic life."

NICOLE WILLIAMS, career expert; bestselling author, *Wildly Sophisticated, Earn What You're Worth,* and *Girl on Top*

"Dr. Sandra Parker's whole brain approach speaks to the intellect and then leads us to our hearts where our sage self lives. Embracing unrest is our key to unlocking the gift of feeling and accessing our true brilliance. A must-read for those who are ready to live life fully."

ERNA HAGGE, president, Hagge Global Institute; executive coach and organizational development consultant; author, *Tri-Namics*

"If you have ever experienced a gap between what you long for and the reality of life, this call to embrace unrest and feel the depth of your emotion is a manifesto for being fully alive. Dr. Parker reveals the many ways we all numb and disconnect from genuine feeling. And yet, page by page, she shares a methodical roadmap detailing how to work with all feelings big and small to become more authentic, resilient, and connected. Embracing unrest is the alchemy for transforming adversity into blessing and chaos into meaning. This book is a thrilling journey into the possible."

JUSTINE COHEN, founder, DownUnder School of Yoga

embracing
*un*rest

harness vulnerability
to tame anxiety
and spark growth

embracing
*un*rest

SANDRA PARKER PhD

PAGE TWO

The epigraph, the poem "Boundaries" © 1995,
appears by permission of Lynn Ungar.

Although lessons learned from the treatment of
actual patients are included in the patient stories,
the historical events and facts represented have
been changed to protect the identities of any real
patients and to protect their confidentiality.
For example, the names, ages, careers, backgrounds,
the number and sex of their children, as well as
other details of their histories have been deliberately
altered. Consequently, all characters appearing
in this book are fictitious. Any resemblance to real
persons, living or dead, is purely coincidental.

The information provided in this book is not
intended to be a substitute for professional medical
advice, diagnosis, or treatment that can be provided
by your own physician, psychologist, psychiatrist,
or other mental health practitioner. If you have any
specific concerns about your mental health, you
should consult your doctor or therapist. Do not use
this information in lieu of professional advice given
by qualified medical professionals and do not
disregard professional medical advice or delay seeking
professional advice because of information you have
read in this book.

Cataloguing in publication information is available
from Library and Archives Canada.
ISBN 978-1-77458-281-7 (paperback)
ISBN 978-1-77458-282-4 (ebook)

Page Two
pagetwo.com

Developmental editing by Scott Steedman
Edited by Kendra Ward
Cover design by Taysia Louie
Interior design by Cameron McKague

drsandraparker.com

To the intelligent animal of your body,
calling you home to this shimmering moment.

"Listen. Every molecule is
humming its particular pitch.
Of course you are a symphony.
Whose tune do you think the
planets are singing as they dance?"

LYNN UNGAR, "BOUNDARIES"

contents

introduction

*"A world lives within you. No one else
can bring you news of this inner world."*
JOHN O'DONOHUE

"I CAN'T BREATHE!" Maya said, eyes wide scanning the
room frantically for an exit, "there's not enough air." The
room was cavernous, big institutional windows, high
ceilings, and bright linoleum floors. We were in Sherbrooke
Centre, the since-demolished home of the psychiatry depart-
ment at Royal Columbian Hospital in New Westminster,
British Columbia, and I was an intern facilitating a group for
people with panic disorder, alongside my clinical supervisor.

We had come to the most difficult part of the program,
when people tuned in to their bodies as we evoked sensations
that would resemble panic episodes. We ran on the spot until
our hearts were pounding, spun in desk chairs until the room
was reeling, and sucked in deep, fast breaths until a cascade
of lightheadedness, shortness of breath, and tingling signaled
hyperventilation. And now, despite having more than enough

oxygen in the room and in her bloodstream, Maya wanted to escape the room and the feelings in her body.

I touched her hand, looked into her eyes, and asked if she would let me stay with her and see what might happen if she didn't avoid her experience. She was trembling and her hand was cold, but she blinked and nodded yes. I asked her to notice, just notice, what was happening inside. Her gaze shifted to the door, and I assured her, "Of course you can leave if you want to. But if you want to find out what is happening inside you, maybe you could stay here with me and feel it?"

Maya described her tight chest and dizziness and her impulse to gasp for air. "You're not in danger. These are feelings, so could we stay right here in all this discomfort and see what happens?" She looked at me like I was a lunatic, but I didn't budge and neither did she. In that moment Maya did what doesn't come naturally—she turned *toward* her vulnerable experience. Rather than avoid or distract or tell herself scary stories, Maya turned inward to experience her uncomfortable sensations.

A moment passed, then two, as her trembling slowed, and her body settled. Her shoulders dropped, her chest softened, and she exhaled. She checked through her body and shook her head as though in disbelief. She lifted her head with a perplexed smile and said, "I'm okay." I smiled and nodded, but she said again, "No, I really mean it. I am okay! I thought I was going to suffocate. I thought I was going to die, but I am really okay."

As she began to look around the room, I urged Maya to keep her inner focus and stay a little longer with her body as it registered her loving attention. She was quiet for several minutes then said in a clear, confident voice, "This is new. That feeling always seemed more than I could manage. I've told myself stories and tried to run away from that feeling for so long. And I don't need to. I don't need to leave the room and I don't need to leave what I feel. I can stay with myself and make the bad feeling better. That's so weird, but it feels good to be here, connected. Actually, I feel more like me."

That moment was powerful for Maya and an epiphany for me. I was witnessing something profoundly human, not only for people who suffer with panic, but for all of us. In the cognitive-behavioral framework my supervisor worked within, what we were doing is called *interoceptive exposure*. "Interoception" means "internal perception," using your inner senses to detect physical sensations on the inside, like being able to notice you are hungry or tired or tense. Doing the exercises produced panic-like feelings to "desensitize" people so they no longer reacted to sensations they associated with panic episodes and had come to fear.

But engaging more deeply with our bodies in those vulnerable moments, like Maya did, like I and so many others I've worked with over the decades have done, is not "desensitizing." It is coming home. Filled with surprise and gratitude in these interoceptive homecomings, we remember our deepest selves and access the resources and gifts we find there.

Vulnerability and Unrest

As an intern I glimpsed for the first time a hidden predicament we all share that is at the heart of our troubles. In my thirty years of helping people, I have come to see how what troubles you arises from everything you do, consciously or not, to avoid experiencing the vulnerability of your inner life. Anxiety, intimacy problems, and depression are all experience-avoidance problems.

What do I mean by "experiencing the vulnerability of your inner life"? I mean slowing down and feeling in your body as your longing stirs and bumps up against your limits.

You are always vulnerable, with limits to your control over things that matter to you. That is a fact of life. But that abiding fact becomes an immediate experience when you want things to be a certain way (perhaps calm, happy, healthy, predictable, or not panicky) and are confronted with the reality that you can't just make it so. You're not the ultimate boss of very much at all. Whether you want things to stay the same or to change, whether you want things to hurry up or slow down, your control has limits. Even your feelings are not yours to control. When your heart swells as you hear a beautiful piece of music or quivers as you await news of a friend's diagnosis, when it feels like it will break as you see a baby bird fallen from its nest or fires up when you recognize you cannot make your neighbor treat his dog better, an inner force moves you whether you want it to or not. And in that vulnerable moment, a jolt of energy unsettles you.

That disruptive energy is *unrest*, a sharp spike of nervous system arousal heralding a phenomenon filled with uncertainty. Unrest announces the optimal moment to tune in and spark your growth. *And here is our shared predicament: the brain unconsciously misinterprets unrest's nervous system activation and reacts as if there were danger.* You are wired to avoid danger, so your brain's misinterpretation makes you flee yourself in that moment. You disconnect, distract, shut down, avoid, or get overwhelmed. So, although unrest invites you home to feel and grow, you unknowingly misread the invitation as a threat and avoid your experience.

Experience Avoidance

Maybe you are thinking, "But I don't avoid my experience. I do what I want and know what I feel, and I can tell you what's important, or if I'm happy or sad or enjoying something." But *doing* something or *knowing* something isn't *experiencing* something. Your idea about what you are experiencing is not your experience; it is at least one step removed and many degrees less vulnerable.

Unrest is invisible to most of us. It happens fast, and we usually react to it without ever registering the feeling. When unrest stirs, some people react fearfully and make up scary stories to explain their agitated feeling. Those people look "anxious." Others react by tuning out, having learned to compartmentalize and deny vulnerability. Those people would never think of themselves as anxious, yet they avoid discomfort that they do not even acknowledge. Whether catastrophizing or ignoring unrest, people suffer when they miss the benevolent, growth-promoting opportunity in its call. "Fear of fear" is at the root of panic disorder. But it is also at the root of what's going on for *all of us* when we are touched by the truth of our vulnerability. It is simply the human condition. We are all wired to move away from the discomfort of unrest.

The world moves faster and faster. At this speed it's hard to see how much you live in your ideas of life, how avoidant of in-the-moment feelings you are. Experience has a continuum of intensity, so it might make sense to you how intense events like the death of a loved one could feel "too much" and prompt you to avoid your inner life, but you might not see how you habitually miss out on subtle moments that could foster your growth. You can see a house on fire but not a candle flickering.

Are you free to follow your dreams or hampered by self-doubt? Can you stay present in the moment, or are you tormented by worry or regret or a frantic need to keep busy? Must you have control and certainty in order to cope? Or can you tolerate the inevitable ambiguity of life? Can you ask for help, or does that make you feel weak? Do you feel hopeless or self-attacking when faced with your human vulnerability? Does it seem like you ought to feel more joy than you do? Or can you laugh and cry and feel hope and act assertively to change? Can you let in the love of others? Can you connect with the larger world and feel engaged and empowered to make a difference? Are you living the meaningful life you long for? Or have you settled for getting by? The answers to your questions are inside you, heralded by a tiny signal, easy to miss, that holds the key to your growth.

The Physiology of Emotional Growth

Maya's reaction was so intense that trying to avoid what she felt made sense to her—and probably would to you, too. Yet staying present to unrest in her body was life affirming and growth promoting for Maya. Similarly, imagine your sister telling you she has just had a miscarriage. Your spike of unrest might unconsciously prompt you to brace against what you feel and to distract your sister from her pain. Yet when you understand the wisdom of unrest as your call to come home in a precise moment of vulnerability, you soothe your body and bear your grief and offer true compassion as your sister feels her pain and knows she is not alone.

But what about a more neutral experience like a walk in the woods. How might you avoid fully drinking that in? And how could that ordinary experience foster growth? You might walk through the woods and miss the experience, so caught up in distracting thoughts that when your companion mentions she has spotted a strange purplish fungus at the base of a tree for the third time, you say, "What fungus?" You have not really seen anything at all. Or you could be mindfully aware of the experience, saying, "Yeah, that fungus is cool." You are noticing, yes, but avoiding how the experience moves you. Or what if you open to your experience when unrest disrupts you? As you tune in and soothe your body with warm attention, your everyday awareness is opened to the joyous profusion of nature. You are moved by the alien beauty of the fungus, perhaps humbled by awe, or grateful to your legs for transporting you there. You sense how, when you embrace unrest, you are safe enough to feel what is "out there" "in here."

Unrest invites you into a life of transcendent richness via a small shift in your nervous system. This is the physiology of emotional growth. Do you notice and soothe the spike of unrest when it disrupts you? Do you stay with your experience, willing to be surprised by its nature and scope, and vulnerably go where it means to take you? Or are you skittering on the surface of your experience, rushing along ticking off boxes or preoccupied by stories that remove you from the immediacy of the moment? Coming home is not easy, but any experience you illuminate with your wholehearted, undivided attention transcends your cognitive grasp and takes you deeper into the realms of your authentic, resilient self.

Maya and Me (and You)

How much of your inner life can you intimately know? At Royal Columbian Hospital, I arrived as an intern out of touch with the truth of my feelings. It wasn't always that way. My mother said her pregnancy with me, the third of her four daughters, was among the happiest times of her life. She was hopeful and radiant, and I was the happiest baby she'd ever seen, easy to soothe and delighting in every aspect of being alive, save being clothed. The only time I cried, she said, was when she dressed me. I entered this life wanting to feel everything.

But within six months my mother was pregnant with my baby sister, and my parents' marriage had hit the skids. They were fighting, and my mother had morning sickness and had begun smoking cigarettes to give herself energy and calm her nerves. My sweet sister Carol was born with colic and could not stop crying. Our charismatic, womanizing, intelligent father began drinking more heavily, and his temper got worse. Money was short and nerves were frayed. My mother tried so hard to take care of us but couldn't seem to love herself enough to come out from behind the Plexiglas wall that kept her at a distance from her life, and us.

When I was five my parents divorced; my father fled the province and all responsibility for us, and my mother was an exhausted, single working mother of four. I grew up with antennae that tracked my mother's pain and a nervous system that knew how to conform around her needs. If my mother tried to be good, I tried to be perfect. My purpose was to make others feel better.

By the time I was a psychology intern, I'd rescued my husband from his totalitarian homeland as he immigrated to Canada, and I was working to support us until he could finish his medical training. My wake-up call came as I was working with Maya and others in the panic program, when my husband broke the news of his six-month-old baby with his receptionist. My good-girl halo shattered along with all the stories I told myself about my wonderful marriage and life. It was time to experience the truth.

Even though Maya with her panic disorder seemed to be in worse shape than I was, she and I were no different really.

I looked good, appeared competent, was coping on the outside, excelling in school and supporting others. But stories I told myself were making me sick. Maya told herself, "I'm going to die" rather than feel what her body was feeling. I told myself, "There's nothing wrong, I'm fine, my marriage is fine, I'm happy" rather than face the pain of rejection and loneliness. For years I had unconsciously misread my body's signals as danger, ignoring myself by overworking, prioritizing my husband's needs, and numbing myself with food. In facing the truth of my inner experience, just as for Maya, I accessed my resilience and emerged more authentic and alive.

This being human gig is not easy. Experiencing vulnerability is daunting, and that is not your fault. You are infused with your soul's hunger to experience life. You are embodied so you can touch and taste and smell and hear and see and feel the miraculous world in which you are manifest. But being alive is vulnerable; at some point you and me and all of us will die. So, you are also charged with a protective energy meant to prevent you from simply flying off a cliff edge just for the rush of being alive, since you would not be, for very long. You inherit this tension between longing for experience and limits to experience—between your soul's longing to devour everything and your body's need to keep you safe. This is not pathology. It is not weakness. It is simply human.

But as our world has become ever-more complex and digital and technological, the needle has tilted away from an even balance between experiencing and safety, to where we are mistaking vulnerability for danger. We are avoiding our inner lives as though our feelings were saber-toothed tigers. Experience phobia is at the heart of our suffering, creating an epidemic of anxiety and apathy as we rush to distract and numb ourselves so as not to feel.

"A world lives within you. No one else can bring you news of this inner world."

JOHN O'DONOHUE

We have become restricted by conservative unconscious processes meant to protect us from physical harm and death, so now our guarded mind rules us, compelling us to avoid not only that which would harm or kill us, but also the simple vulnerability of what it means to be alive. That protective reflex removes us from what we feel even before we know we feel it.

Our minds, in their overabundance of caution, have shrunk our lives and made it seem better to live in our ideas about being alive than to inhabit the immediate flow of living. Of course, we must also take care of our precious, tender bodies. But we do not need to live detached from them. Our souls call on us to live while we're alive.

Embracing Unrest

This book is a guide and an invitation, a support as you do the brave work of moving your personal needle of human tension to the center, balanced between experiencing everything and not risking life and limb in the process, so you can open yourself to the authentic and powerful life you are meant to live. This book shows you how to recognize your spike of unrest as it heralds the optimal moment for tuning in and feeling your inner life. You will learn how to differentiate unrest from other experiences, and how to embrace it so you can ride waves of emotion to new shores of yourself.

In each chapter there are stories from my clinical practice and from my own life to illuminate how paying inner attention is your path to the rich, spacious, and authentic life you long for. Each chapter also includes practices for embodying the principles shared throughout the book. This is not a cognitive journey. I will say it again: growth happens through experiencing (and reflecting upon your experiencing). Practice and reflect upon those activities and you will gain freedom to know yourself more deeply, bounce back from difficulty more easily, and connect with others more intimately.

Chapter one unveils the inner workings of your powerful, hidden force for transformation: unrest. You will see into the enigma of personal growth: how unrest calls you home to the optimal moment for growth but also feels like danger, prompting you to avoid your experience and thereby creating your suffering. You will take your first steps to perceive and greet unrest as it calls you. Chapter two sheds light on two other experiences that can be mistaken for unrest: anxiety and fear. Those terms are often used interchangeably, and the lack of clarity has created confusion, so you will learn to discern one from the other and how each needs a different response. Chapter three introduces the practice of interoception and its central role in soothing your body so you can open to your inner life. You will learn how to use your inner senses to perceive tension and agitation in your body, resist the urge to escape your experience, and foster interoceptive homecoming.

Chapter four demystifies the challenge and gift of vulnerability. You will see how, when your longing meets limits, you face the profound, inescapable truth of being human. Although you cannot escape the truth of *being vulnerable*, you can avoid the discomfort of *feeling vulnerable*, but then you find yourself lost and homeless. The secret to coming home and mattering is not denying what you long for, nor giving up when there are limits; the secret is loving yourself in the painful place of "I can't" and discovering what happens next. Chapter five reveals how you journeyed away from your original hunger to feel it all. Three main forces contribute to your aversion to deeply experiencing, and you will find greater self-compassion as you come to understand the heroic challenge of staying close to the vulnerable truth of being human.

Chapter six offers a roadmap for coming home, with clear instructions for how to pay attention to your body to soothe unrest and guidelines for how to be optimally effective. Chapter seven teaches you about the wavelike flow of emotion that aims to lift and carry you to the riches of your inner resources. I illustrate how information and energy coded in emotion helps you adapt to reality and grow capacities for a bigger, more resilient life. Chapter eight illustrates tricksters in your psyche that want to remove you from what you feel. Those exits from the truth are called defenses, and this chapter identifies defensive patterns of behavior so you can know when you have abandoned yourself. Chapter nine shows how to take the fruit of your loving inner efforts and offer them outward to the world as you bring your well-regulated nervous system to bear on challenges we all face. You will behold how your capacity to soothe unrest and access emotion empowers you in intimate relationships, in the workplace, and inspiring change in the larger world. Chapter ten reminds you unrest is something you already experience and react to, but without conscious knowledge. It encourages you to be patient and compassionate toward yourself as you awaken to unrest's invitation to matter.

Your mind and feelings and senses are all servants of your soul's hunger for experiencing life, meant to provide you with the richest adventure in creativity. You are wired with a miraculous signal designed to get your attention in the optimal moment to foster growth.

Are you ready to give up the stories about your life and tune in to life itself? I want to help you feel safe enough to *be* here. Let's begin this journey now together as you use your inner senses to recognize and embrace the spike of unrest as your call to growth, so you can become fully authentic, resilient, and connected, and give your gifts to the world.

1

embracing unrest

*"When a great moment knocks on the door of your life
it is often no louder than the beating of your own heart,
and it is very easy to miss it."*

BORIS PASTERNAK

ARON'S FAVORITE expression was "I've got this!" I could feel the exclamation mark in his tone of voice on our initial phone call, when he explained how his physician believed his gastrointestinal difficulties might be associated with stress. "My doctor doesn't have a clue. I'm not stressed. I exercise, I eat well, I have hobbies, I play guitar. I've got this!"

Aaron was the executive director for a large seniors' care home corporation, and he loved his work. He managed a large team, mentoring and monitoring and handling crises. He was known as someone who listened to his team and incorporated feedback. However, the demands at work were coming faster and faster and the responsibilities weighed heavier each year. His work had no boundaries; he went to bed with his phone beside him and it was the first thing he looked at when he opened his eyes. He had no complaints to speak of. But for the past few years his gut was chronically upset, with bouts of bloating and gas and cramping for which no manner of testing could find an organic cause.

When I met Aaron, I noticed his left leg bouncing slightly as he sat across from me, and his fingers were tapping. I asked him what he would like help with, and he said he wanted me to give him "a clean bill of psychological health" so his doctor would stop pressing him to take care of his stress. I asked him if he was aware of his leg bouncing and his fingers tapping, and Aaron blew those off, "I always do that. It doesn't mean anything."

When I asked what it was like to have no medical explanation for his gastrointestinal distress, he became visibly annoyed. "I just need a medical treatment for my gut, and everything will be good."

"It must be hard not to have certainty or control over your symptoms," I said softly. "You are used to having answers and solving problems. It's not easy to be confronted with vulnerability."

I explained how his body was talking to him through his nervous system, trying to get his attention with unrest. "You mean I could be anxious and not even know it? What?!" I asked him if he'd noticed any other clues and, upon reflection, he said he hadn't been sleeping so well and some colleagues had recently mentioned him being more impatient.

I told him he needed to be the executive director of his body and really listen to its feedback. This was a new idea for Aaron, whose relationship with his body (if he thought of it at all) consisted not of listening but telling it what to do. He dismissed his inner experience so quickly he had no idea how agitated and tense he was. Instead, he pushed and ignored and denied what he felt. He blamed himself and was hard on others when things didn't go as planned. Aaron had no room for uncertainty or limits when he wanted something done. He was unaware that his body was in a state of high alert, in an unsustainable, gut-wrenching place.

Sophia was a seasoned physiotherapist with an open smile and long raven hair who came into my office for help with anxiety. Her voice was low and soft, but her graceful, slim body was braced as she described her troubles. "I am too uptight. I haven't slept properly in years. I wake up at night and just can't get back to sleep. My body feels on guard most of the time. I get thinking about certain difficulties in my life and I can't let go; my mind is like a dog with a bone."

I invited Sophia to notice her tension right in the moment. "I've done that. I do all that. Mindfulness and breathing. I meditate and do yoga. Body-awareness stuff is not the help I need." Sophia's idea about herself was more real to her than her experience. She thought of herself as someone who was tuned in to her body. But the problem wasn't a lack of attention, it was that she only checked in to "fix" the anxiety, to "make it go away." And now she had come to me for help to make it go away. "If this therapy doesn't work, then I'm finally just going to go on medication. I deserve to feel better than this."

"You absolutely deserve to feel better," I said gently. "And feeling better starts with actually feeling. Feeling without an agenda. Feeling with the only focus being to allow the experience of what you feel. Feeling without trying to control what happens inside. Without needing the discomfort to go away."

For Sophia, though she was skilled at focusing awareness, her unconscious rejection of uncomfortable feelings in her body prompted her to dismiss my invitation to tune in. Her habit was to pay attention from a safe distance in her head and not surrender to the immediacy of the vulnerable sensations that didn't feel good. She believed she was feeling her body, but she was only observing her feeling. And as a result, she also suffered with awful indecision and difficulties letting herself be close to others. But for Sophia, those problems were unrelated to her disconnection from her body; in fact, she didn't think she was disconnected. She just needed her body to stop feeling bad. Sophia was arguing with reality, feeling she should be a certain way and trying to get control and certainty in a world that has neither.

Where people like Aaron are out of touch with anxious feelings, folks like Sophia are distressed by them and believe they should be able do something (in themselves or in the world) to not feel that way. Yet unrest was simply alerting both Aaron and Sophia to an optimal moment for growth. When they were thrust up against their limits, a deep intelligence inside them spiked unrest to get their attention so they could ride waves of emotion and adapt. But when that great moment knocked on the door, they missed it. Unrest feels uncomfortable, so they did the natural thing and disconnected from it. They pushed and compartmentalized and worried, and unwittingly created misery to avoid feeling discomfort. They missed out on the waves of emotion meant to carry them to greater authenticity, resilience, and connection. But it didn't have to be so.

The Power of Emotion

Provincial health officer Bonnie Henry was standing at the podium, facing bright lights and cameras, microphones, and reporters. As she gave her briefing in the early days of COVID-19 in British Columbia, her low-pitched voice had the slightest quiver and it seemed her mouth was dry. She inhaled small breaths as she spoke of the need to physically distance and protect others, especially the vulnerable elderly. Then, mid-sentence, for fourteen seconds, she was quiet as tears rimmed her eyes and waves of sadness curved through her body. In a moment that was reported internationally, she allowed herself to be touched by the truth of her emotion, and in doing so she touched us all. And at that moment we took her hand and accepted her leadership.

The health minister beside her said kindly, but unnecessarily, "It's okay." Bonnie Henry seemed to convey that she already knew it was okay, because it was human. She gazed back out at her audience, at all of us, and said, "Excuse me." Not "I'm sorry." She did not apologize, choke up, sob uncontrollably, or flee the podium. Nor did she flatten herself, speak robotically, or minimize the gravity of her message.

Bonnie Henry embodied the practices that foster emotional maturation. As unrest heralded her point of contact with vulnerability, she slowed down and tuned inward. She gave herself time; a full fourteen seconds passed while cameras and people waited. She tended to the unrest in her body, exhaled, and lightly shook her head. She kept her eyes down to focus internally. She sighed heavily and shrugged her shoulders up and down. Then she looked up and connected with us. We felt her authentic presence. We felt her embrace her own vulnerability as emotion moved her. And we were held also, able to tolerate our own vulnerability just a little bit more, in those uncertain times. We were inspired to be kind, calm, and safe.

Emotions are vulnerable and can be painful. But experiencing emotion fosters growth. Feeling your deepest truth enlivens and matures you. When you can fully feel your emotions, you are more authentic and resilient and can be more intimate with others. Unrest heralds the optimal moment for paying attention to this growth-promoting experience.

You have the answers to your difficulties within yourself. Your emotions are the energy that will propel and transform you. Awakening from the slumber of numbing and distraction takes effort, but you are so very worth it. You deserve to live your most rich and authentic life. And the world needs people who can be themselves, care about others, be moved by the truth, and act in service to the larger whole. It's time to be moved. It's time to wake up and feel your feelings deeply.

So why do you (and me, and most of us) resist the very thing that could hasten the emergence of your authentic self? Because when emotion is triggered, the feeling I call *unrest* disturbs you. And unfortunately, unrest feels like danger.

The Enigma of Personal Growth

Your wise body uses unrest to pinpoint the optimal moment to tune inward to foster your growth. Unrest signals vulnerability, the moment you bump up against limits to control over things that matter to you. Your tightening right shoulder grips—and, instead of ignoring it, you pause, paying careful attention to the tense muscles. After a moment of warm interest, your muscles release and you feel your shoulder drop slightly. Your body registers your awareness and settles, allowing a channel to open within you. A wave of sadness comes through, carrying you to a truth you have been avoiding. You realize you are working so hard to get everything done, but you cannot do it all alone. You wish you were more efficient and had more time and energy and did not have human limits.

But you are indeed only human. The sadness rises and a heavy pressure pulls on your sternum. You breathe into the feeling as it crests and then ebbs, and you find a space inside yourself where you matter. You accept yourself in your limits. You feel less alone, more capable of giving yourself patience and compassion, and more able to ask for help.

Unrest bids you awaken to cocreate your life. But there is a paradox that makes tuning in to unrest a radical act. Unrest uses the same quick signaling system as fear, which makes it

"There's no 'should' or 'should not' when it comes to having feelings. They're part of who we are and their origins are beyond our control."

FRED ROGERS

feel like danger, something to avoid. Unrest chimes, "Tune in and pay attention." But it sends that message through survival circuitry that warns, "Run away!"

You see the dilemma. The emotion meant to grow you evokes a reflex to protect you. Without realizing, you disengage from what you feel. Instead of embracing unrest so you can experience emotion and become more yourself, you escape. You distract and worry and shut down and turn against yourself. Your hunger to flourish bumps up against an impulse to protect, and the unconscious struggle manifests as depression, anxiety, and disconnection from yourself and others.

This is the enigma of personal growth: You must do the opposite of what comes naturally. Rather than brace against unrest, you must embrace it in your body when it rouses you.

We live in a world of overwhelm, riddled with distraction and addiction. We are entertaining ourselves to death, so we don't have to feel. We gobble anxiety medications like candy while an opioid epidemic fills our emergency rooms. We jeopardize lives on the road because we cannot put our phones away. We are devouring the earth's resources in an insatiable compulsion to fill our inner emptiness. We numb ourselves because we are too afraid to face what reality stirs in us.

But our denial is deadly. Disconnected from vital emotional information, we inhabit the shadows of our own lives as our communities fracture and the earth weeps. Some of us are haunted by the growing knowledge that we cannot continue this way. Our nerves are frazzled, our hearts hungry, and our bodies worn with the neglect of our inner lives. We must stop turning away from the truth, and the painful emotion that accompanies it.

Emotion links you with reality. It lets you know *that* you are touched by life and *how* you are touched by life. This happens whether you want it to or not. You do not create your emotions—they happen to you. Your emotions are triggered by people, thoughts, memories, events, sights and smells, and all sorts of stimuli; but your emotional reaction has its own life. It is your unique activation arising out of the "who" of you: your temperament, history, appraisal, current state, and understanding. Your emotional reactions are at the heart of your authentic self. Put me in front of a romantic movie and I might be annoyed, while you might sob your guts out. My inner emotional biosphere moves me, and yours moves you, in ways we may never fully comprehend.

Emotion flows through you as an embodied vital force. It comes before words. You feel emotion first as a physical experience and, as you're being moved (if you are aware of your body's activation), translate it into words. Even our language reveals how you are acted upon by emotion: you *are moved*. You do not move yourself; the wave of feeling moves you. This does not make you weak, but it does reveal you as vulnerable. Feeling an unbidden force moving powerfully through your own body is an immediate and intimate experience that shatters the illusion that you are "in control."

Despite how vulnerable you may feel when emotion stirs, it strengthens you to face the challenges of reality and adapt. In the middle of yet another argument with your brother about his drinking, he rolls his eyes and tells you to stop making a big deal about nothing. He's just lost his driver's license and his employer has put him on notice. You feel your arms trembling with tension and you're holding your breath. Instead of ignoring yourself and pushing through to make your point, you notice the bracing in your body, you stop, and you slowly exhale. In that moment you see how your anger and need to help are covering up the painful, terrible truth of your sorrow. You stop arguing with him and let your eyes fill with tears. Your grief is the truth; you cannot control his choices. Rather than reject yourself in your human limits, you allow the wave of sadness to crest and carry you to a new place where you feel your love for your brother and your acceptance of yourself. Your grief helps you let go of the fight to "fix" him and opens a loving space in your heart for him. As you open to your feelings, you come to terms with what you cannot change, and you change what you can. So, although you cannot control emotion, you can lean toward it and make the most of it to grow.

A Wake-Up Call from Your Soul

As you are faced with vulnerability, a wake-up call from your soul rouses you and the call of unrest is ringing under your skin, calling you home.

Emotion and unrest accompany each other as two distinct forces in your body. To harness their vital power, you must learn to notice and differentiate them. You are waiting for your friend at a restaurant, and she is late, as usual. You can think of half-a-dozen times when she has left you waiting for twenty minutes or more, but you've always smiled and accepted her breezy excuses. Now your butt is clenched, and your toes are tapping as your fingers fidget with the napkin. In the past you might have ignored these sensations and used the anxious discomfort as a jumping off point for worrying about why she's late: "Is she in a car accident?" "Did I mess up the time?" "Is it just me? Am I so boring?"

Instead, today you notice unrest and, instead of going to your old stories, tune in and carefully feel your body's agitation until it settles. You become aware of heat in your core and a strengthening and lengthening in your spine, and you realize you feel annoyed. The truth calms you. You feel motivated to speak up when she arrives, to let her know you want her to be more respectful of your time. You feel unrest wanting to rise again and you soothe it once more—tending to your feeling of vulnerability is a dynamic process. You sense the time has come for you to assert yourself and be more authentic. You see being honest with your friend can help your relationship become a safer, closer bond. Emotion is the energy propelling your growth, and unrest is the inkling (invisible and misunderstood) that emotion is surfacing.

Unrest alerts you like the ringing of your phone. Your muscles brace and tighten, your heart beats faster, your breath speeds up, adrenaline flows through your bloodstream and you feel agitated. Just as your body tenses and you have the urge to avoid all the fuss, a doorway opens to your biggest life. Walking through that door means slowing down and paying attention to unrest so you can soothe the body and access the power of your emotions.

Many of us divide emotions into good or bad. Joy, love, and hope are viewed as good. Anger, guilt, and sadness are seen as bad. But emotion is a paradox. All emotions are "good" as they inform and motivate us, and they all can feel "bad" as they stir unrest. We need to accept this mixture of good and bad. Rather than brace against unrest, we need to heed its call and embrace it with warm attention to access the transmuting truth of our feelings.

Embracing Unrest in Your Longing and Your Limits

The pain and beauty of the present moment are not more than you can bear. Your experience avoidance arises from an old reflex that expects you will not be able to cope with what it feels like to be vulnerably human. You are born with a radiant energy that wants to animate and create and evolve and feel it all, and the world is structured with limits that protect and contain and obstruct you. You are limitless love reaching for creation. Poised between your longing as it pulls you toward all that inspires you and the limiting structures of reality that hold you back, your vulnerability feels intolerable, and your reflex is to avoid.

That unconscious habit must be brought into awareness and the old pathways rewired to free yourself from the prison of numbing and worry and distraction. You have the seeds of your emergence within, in your hunger to live your most meaningful and vital life. And the technology for your growth is wired into your own body, in the unrest you feel when faced with vulnerability. You are meant to register unrest so that you can tune attention inward. As you deepen your capacity to notice and soothe unrest, you open to your emotions, and they can do their transformational work carving deeper and deeper channels for experiencing life. You deserve to matter. It's time to live your most authentic, resilient, and connected life.

This is a love story—with yourself. It is a story of one choice: love or fear. You can embrace what you feel and grow, or you can avoid what you feel and abandon your full potential in this life. This is not an easy choice. Tuning in to unrest is unfamiliar and doesn't immediately feel good. But you are meant to encounter the catalyst of unrest as it sparks your growth and deepens your capacity for being fully alive.

The Problem with Anxiety

Although anxiety and unrest feel the same in your body, they are not the same thing at all. Unrest signals your point of contact with vulnerability. Your nervous system is calling you to approach your inner experience. But unrest feels like threat. Most of the time when it rings, you don't consciously register it and, without realizing, you run away.

Anxiety is something different. It is the avoidant thing you do *after* unrest stirs you. It is your exit from the immediate physical discomfort of unrest. No one *wants* to feel a knot in their stomach or braced muscles or shallow breathing or sweaty palms or a dry mouth or a quaking in their legs. In fact, your brain misreads these signals as danger, and you are wired to move away. So, when unrest signals emotion, you abandon yourself to anxiety by engaging in movies and stories and avoidant behaviors to escape or make sense of the feeling of threat. You leave the present moment and worry about the future or ruminate about the past, or criticize yourself, or distract yourself with swipes and clicks and a glass of wine. Those exits are anxiety.

Without registering your fidgety hands or tight shoulders or held breath (never mind the riches of emotion beneath), you grab a bag of cheese puffs or launch into worry movies in your mind or scan your Instagram or Facebook feeds. Or you may notice discomfort but, instead of tuning in, tell stories of danger ("There's something wrong with me; I'm going to pass out") or weakness ("I'm a coward; people will judge me").

Your anxious stories and avoidant behaviors *are* anxiety. Anxiety is how you leave your experience of unrest in the here and now. Anxious stories increase physical agitation because your body listens to the messages and gears up to protect you. But there is nothing to protect you from. It is only unrest, meant to help you grow.

Unrest asks you to pay inner attention when vulnerability goes from an idea to an experience. That is not a problem. The real problem is your nervous system is calling to you and you are ignoring it or mistaking the message as danger. Everything you do to escape your experience creates suffering. Unrest wants to bring you home so waves of emotion can carve deeper and deeper channels for living your most authentic life.

PRACTICE: PERCEIVE YOUR CALL OF UNREST

In a few sentences, write down what is troubling you. What moved you to pick up this book? What is the problem *inside you* that you want help with? Think deeply enough so that you can describe your struggle from an internal vantage point, rather than as a problem with a situation or with another person. How is the situation or person creating a problem *inside you*?

Do you spend too much time trying to please others, unable to say no even when you want to? Do you struggle to feel that you matter? Are you anxious and worried? Do you feel irritable a lot of the time? Do you have a hard time deciding? Do you resist change? Are you eating or drinking or spending or distracting yourself more than you want to be? Do you cling anxiously in relationships? Or do you shut down when others try to get close? Do you feel stuck or lacking in motivation or direction? Do you feel drained too much of the time? Do you give up too easily? Or do you push yourself too hard, criticizing your efforts as never good enough?

Now, get your smartphone. No, not to call anyone; you will be listening for the call of unrest. And so you will use the marvelous magic genie that is your phone and with the camera on you and the video recording, you will read aloud your stated problem. Make sure the camera is propped up on something far enough away from you that you can see your whole face and upper body and arms and hands.

Press "record" on your phone's video function and tell the story of your troubles. Talk about what is frustrating you, making you feel alone or hopeless or overwhelmed or shut down. Describe in some detail how it is a problem for you. Then give a specific example of how that happens in your life. If you are talking about having trouble with procrastination, give an example of how you intended to sit down and write that chapter and found yourself cleaning out your desk drawers (okay, you're right, that one is mine). Describe your example in as much detail as possible, saying what you were thinking and feeling and doing.

As you speak aloud to the camera, observe if you are bracing, holding your breath, fidgeting, or clenching. Once you have shared a clear and thorough description of your trouble, stop the video and pause for a moment. Close your eyes and let yourself be aware of what you feel, having spoken so vulnerably about something that is not working the way you want in your life right now.

Now, play the video back. Give yourself the gift of your undivided attention. Expect there might be a part of you that wants to judge, a part that comments on your voice or your appearance or your "performance," and gently but firmly ask that part to go for a walk and let you do this work in the safety of warm eyes that do not judge you.

Feel how vulnerability *activates* your body. That experience of unrest is what you are wired to avoid. This is brave. You are going against your habitual nervous system reaction and a lifetime of ignoring yourself. Watch yourself carefully and see if you can observe your body even more closely in the video. Can you notice a furrowed brow? Are your fingers fidgety? Are your shoulders up? Are you pulling in and making yourself small? Is your mouth tight or pursed? Play the video a few times to make sure you have caught all the signals of unrest that you can see.

Pay attention to your body on the video without judgment (as best you can), and without attempting to fix or change anything. You have declared a problem, and that is a courageous step. Unrest signaled you, letting you know there is emotion flowing underneath your words. No need to know yet what the emotion is. You are just naming the problem and noticing unrest.

Can you let yourself matter right there in your discomfort? Even for a breath? You have perceived your call of unrest. That is success.

2

differentiating unrest, anxiety, and fear

"Who's not sat tense before his own heart's curtain?"
RAINER MARIA RILKE

LIKE DOROTHY in *The Wizard of Oz*, to follow your inner yellow brick road home, you must be curious about the characters you'll meet along the way and learn which to draw near and which to give wide berth to. That's not easy, because unrest, anxiety, and fear are *identical in their physiology*. They all activate the same nervous system pathway in your body. They all feel the same. They differ, though, in their origin and purpose, and this difference is *everything*. Let's take a closer look at these three stirrings of your nervous system. But first we need a (very) short lesson in physiology.

Unrest, anxiety, and fear are all manifestations of nervous system arousal. Threaded through you are neural pathways, like shimmering filaments, weaving connections between your brain and your body. Your *central nervous system*, your brain and spinal cord, exchanges information through chemicals and electrical impulses along those living pathways to and from your muscles and organs, in your *peripheral nervous system.*

Your peripheral nervous system has two parts: autonomic and somatic.

Your *autonomic nervous system* regulates things like your heartbeat, breathing, and digestion without engaging your conscious mind. Your autonomic nervous system is divided into three parts: *sympathetic*, *parasympathetic*, and *enteric*. Without getting too complicated, you can think of your sympathetic nervous system as a quick animating force that mobilizes your body for action and the parasympathetic system as a dampening force to bring your reactions back to baseline. The enteric system is a network of neurons within the smooth muscle wall of the gastrointestinal tract that controls digestive functions like blood flow, the uptake of nutrients, and motility. The central nervous system and enteric nervous system share many common neurotransmitters, which is why the gut is sometimes referred to as our second brain, and how we have ways of sensing things "in our gut."

Your *somatic nervous system* involves the striated or skeletal muscles that move your body in space and support you. These are the muscles you can voluntarily move, which is why they are also termed *voluntary muscles.* You can consciously control the somatic nervous system, sending a command down through the *efferent* pathway to ask your arm to reach for that mug of beer or ask your leg to lift higher to step over that sleeping dog. Your voluntary muscles relay information back up to your brain through *afferent* nerve pathways, letting you know that mug of beer is heavy, and that dog is taller than you realized, so maybe don't take a swig of beer while trying to clamber over the dog.

Your autonomic and somatic nervous systems chat away like magpies all day and all night to your central nervous system. Electrical and chemical messages arising from information gleaned by your sense organs (eyes, ears, nose, tongue, and skin) and inner senses (your *interoception*, a subtle but powerful capacity that we will discuss in the next chapter) are relayed along neural pathways to the central nervous system, which sends responses back. "Yum, that apple pie smells good!" and "Wow, my mouth is watering now." Your nervous system is your interface with the world, and unrest is a particular manifestation from your nervous system, letting you know that reality has just smacked you upside the head with a limit to your control, even one as small as "I wish I didn't crave that pie right now."

Unrest

Unrest announces your point of contact with vulnerability. It disrupts you. Unrest can nudge you with a quiver or a held breath or it can derail you as your heart pounds, your stomach knots up, and you are tongue-tied. It is a spike of discomfort meant to get your attention at a key moment as your longing bumps up against limits. It is an immediate, sharp signal that you are on the precipice of a choice: tune in and gain access to your inner resources and wisdom or tune out and suffer in all the ways you escape your truth.

All of us are born with longing, a beautiful vitalizing impulse to reach toward and create a fulfilling life. You want things, and you want things to be a certain way. But life itself is filled with limits. You are torn between an impulse to immerse yourself in what it feels like to be here and an impulse to protect yourself from the limits and losses and uncertainties of life. Vulnerability is longing and limits brushing up against each other. That tension is simply part of being alive and human: "I want to land that job; I want him to love me; I want her to respect me; I don't want to get sick; I don't want you to leave me; I want my dog to live forever." And you cannot 100 percent guarantee those outcomes.

Even the sense that you want to be in control of what you feel is a basic longing that will always be met with limits, since you are moved by life in ways you cannot fully predict nor direct. "I don't want to be too hopeful about winning the lottery," "I want to feel more loving toward her," "I wish I weren't so angry with them," and "I don't want to be so sad" illustrate this difficult truth that we feel what we feel, whether we want to acknowledge it or not. When you are faced with any kind of situation where you long for something and are faced with limits to securing it, the ever-present background truth of human vulnerability suddenly becomes an immediate and intimate experience. Unrest spikes up. Your body revs and tenses to let you know an opportunity for growth is at hand.

This happens fast. It can be subtle or hit you in a rush. Your autonomic and somatic nervous systems gear up to get your attention. When unrest hits, you feel more alert, like an animal with its ears pricked, eyes scanning the environment. You feel a buzzing energy of agitation and a sensation of "readiness." You feel fidgety, especially in your hands and feet. Your voluntary muscles (such as the muscles in your arms and legs and hands) tighten. Your bloodstream is awakened as you release hormones, including adrenaline and cortisol. Your heart rate and blood pressure increase, and you may get warm or even sweaty. Your breathing becomes faster and shallower. You may even hold your breath as though bracing for impact. Your body might up the ante to get your attention, by mobilizing your smooth muscles in your guts. Your stomach can churn or feel queasy. You might burp or feel pressure on your bladder or bowel. Your mouth and eyes get dry, and your airways feel restricted.

Although these sensations sound obvious, we typically don't notice them. Our brain is usually oriented outward and busy in the past and future, and our stoic habit to ignore discomfort means we can be taken by surprise by our feelings, not realizing we've been annoyed or sad for some time. Most of us chronically tune out unrest and only realize something's up when its spike gets so high it dams the rising wave of emotion. If we don't tune in, we can feel flooded or overwhelmed, with a sudden impulse to get it out (yell, leave the room, pace, throw a pencil) or push it in (criticize ourselves, numb out, worry, distract).

The earlier you notice unrest, the easier it is to soothe. And soothing is your job; it's how you show yourself you matter and deliberately foster your emotional development. You can even use small stirrings to strengthen your capacity to feel and deal, the way you might use light weights at the gym.

Unrest is an experience in the here and now, in your body. It is not an idea or a thought, nor a past event or a future dream or a nightmare. It is a physical experience that is inviting you home *right now*, so you can harness the transforming power of your emotion and grow.

Anxiety

We are all disrupted by unrest when we're moved by emotion, but we don't all suffer anxiety. Anxiety is arousal that comes from mental processes, thoughts, stories, and self-judgments, arising *after* unrest signals. Anxiety is how we leave home.

Anxiety can be likened to what Buddhists call "the second arrow." The first arrow is the inevitable emotional pain of life's losses and limits. Although you can't control emotion, you can choose what to do next. If you embrace unrest, you can be carried by healing and time-limited waves of emotion to new shores of yourself and be enriched. If you ignore the first arrow, you can avoid directly experiencing the pain of emotion, but it continues to flow underground, and your avoidance strikes with a second. This is the arrow of endless worry, regret, distraction, disconnection, and numbing. The ways you try to avoid the transitory pain of the first arrow create the interminable suffering that brings people to my office.

Not everyone has a problem with anxiety. We all worry sometimes, but people who relentlessly run scary mental movies and get caught in threatening stories suffer terribly, and they do not have to. There is a path to freedom that travels into the pain and away from suffering. You walk that path by soothing your unrest beneath the anxiety and facing and feeling the emotion your unrest heralds.

While unrest tells you about here and now, anxiety takes you to another place and time. This exit allows you to fantasize that you can control an outcome ("if only," "what if?"). Unfortunately, your anxiety lies to you, and amplifies your bodily arousal. Anxiety is like ignoring your internal alarm clock's friendly message to "wake up" and feel your feelings until the ringing gets so loud that you finally hear it. But then instead of waking up and coming home, you create a story about a fire alarm and tell yourself, "I'm going to die! And it's all my fault! And there's no point in feeling anything at this point anyway."

Imagining awful scenarios is trying to avert something bad by anticipating it. You run a movie anticipating how an upcoming family dinner will play out, and you picture all the ways your siblings might tease you or ignore you or embarrass you, and you see yourself telling them to zip it or bursting into tears or marching out of the room. Your heart is pounding, and your mouth is dry, and the feeling of dread is getting bigger by the hour. But reality is woven with more threads than you could ever snip. You could show up after all that suffering, and everyone is busy with your brother's new puppy. You could spend your entire life running movies with different parameters, trying to predict and eliminate all risk, and you still wouldn't be able to control the outcome with certainty.

Anxious worry is not the same as healthy anticipatory coping, as in preparing for something foreseeable. Christmas always falls on December 25 and so I can look ahead to that date and calculate how much time I will need to buy and wrap presents, how soon I need to send off cards in the mail, and when I need to bake that fruitcake. When you identify a problem and how to respond, you do what you can, and then let it go. You cope. You feel empowered and realistic. Worry, in contrast, is a terrible experience of not being able to let things go. You loop and loop with the same intimidating stories until you are exhausted and disempowered.

Anxiety can also focus on the past. You chew past experiences over and over, second-guessing yourself with the mantra "woulda, shoulda, coulda." You imagine you had the power to do things differently back then, and just *didn't*. You forget who you were and what resources were available at the time. You might tell yourself you are examining this prior experience to ensure you do better next time, but rather than bringing the compassion and curiosity that would make the review a safe opportunity for learning, you torment yourself with a wagging finger and a critical tone.

And speaking of critical voices, anxiety also arises when you judge yourself. When you bombard yourself with "not good enough," "not smart enough," or "not worthy of love," you become anxious. That punishing inner recitation is often the source of the stickiest problems with anxiety— the self-doubt and social inhibition and crippling isolation that can lead folks into depression. Some people are so used to the voice of that inner critic that they don't even hear it— or if they do, they think of it as just "how I am." Some even think that such cruelty makes them perform better. That is never true. No one performs their best when threatened with criticism and rejection. Those messages make our bodies feel even more besieged, and we go into survival mode, all resources oriented to just staying alive.

Despite your unconscious motivation to avoid unrest and make sense of the feeling of threat by telling yourself scary stories, when you escape the truth of your vulnerable emotion, you suffer. When you recognize anxiety's lies, block them, and soothe unrest, you access emotion and grow into all your soul longs for you to be.

Fear

Fear is a core emotion, and although it feels the same as unrest and anxiety in your body, it differs in important ways. Fear tells you about an immediate threat to life and limb and directs you to fight or flee. Fear is critical to survival. Fear organizes your body and your perceptions, orienting you outward to the source of danger as it transforms you into a brilliant organism of escape or attack.

Fear is an ideal response to real, imminent danger. When you're afraid, your body diverts energy from nonemergency processes such as digestion and cell growth to the large muscles of the body, so you are ready to run away from or fight off a predator. Your vision becomes narrow and focused, so you can zero in on the source of danger and identify the best possible escape route. This is what is so perfect about fear: if you are in a life-threatening situation, quickened reactions and strengthened muscles and enhanced lung capacity are lifesaving. Those reactions are not a problem, they are not too much or "stressful." Throwing a hissing rattlesnake off your desk is a fitting response. Throwing your computer off your desk because it keeps freezing is not. (Your frozen computer is not a danger to you. It stirs unrest—you are angry that you just paid a whole lot of money to repair it, and it still isn't working!)

Fear is about the immediate present. If you are afraid of something in the future or the past, you are experiencing anxiety, not fear. Anticipating a dangerous possibility is imagining, not facing, danger. Similarly, recalling a past danger is a memory, not a current threat. You experience fear only when faced with a physical threat right here and now. This is one of the hardest things for chronically anxious people to accept: that their worry is a story, a prediction, a possibility, but it is not *danger*.

Your brain is primed to prioritize the experience of fear. Survival is Mother Nature's number one goal, and fear is her way of telling you that your life is at stake. Fear activates your nervous system and jolts you with the energy, power, and focus to do what you need to do to survive. Fear is your friend and must be obeyed. When in danger, run!

Knowing the Difference

Unrest, anxiety, and fear share underlying circuitry embedded in nervous system pathways that initiate reactions in your body. With all three, your muscles tense and your heart rate and breathing speed up. Even in our language, we often use "anxious," "afraid," "scared," "worried," and "fearful" interchangeably. And although fear and anxiety historically have been conceptualized as arising from different circuitry in the brain, recent neuroimaging research is overturning that idea, showing that the same circuits are activated for both immediate, certain, and uncertain threat (fear and anxiety). That shared physiology is why we so often confuse one for the other. So, although fear and anxiety *are* different, the distinction is not because of a difference in nervous system activation. The difference is in the origin of each experience. When you can identify that difference, you can tailor your response for growth.

Fear is the emotional truth about immediate danger. ("A car is heading straight for me. Jump!") It must be obeyed. Anxiety is a lie told to remove you from the discomfort of unrest. ("If I don't win this project bid, I'm going to die!") It must be blocked so you can access the vulnerable truth underneath. ("I really want this opportunity but can't guarantee it, and that makes me sad.") Unrest signals your point of contact with vulnerability as emotion rises. ("My jaw and my heart are tight because I'm feeling mixed emotions as we disagree. I feel anger/assertion to speak my truth, and I also care about your feelings and value our relationship.") Unrest must be embraced to access your emotional truth and spark growth.

Once you appreciate these distinctions, you can welcome and experience unrest as your counterintuitive and radical path to growth. If you are in immediate danger, orient outward and escape! If you are *not* in immediate danger, orient inward and pay attention to soothe sensations ASAP! If you cannot soothe your arousal, block the stories and criticisms that are freaking your body out! Then pay attention to sensations to soothe your body and access the emotion that will grow you.

Feeling the Difference

The best way to differentiate between unrest, anxiety, and fear is to discover them in yourself. I felt fear, anxiety, and unrest when I sprained my ankle several years ago. It was a lovely, sunny mid-June afternoon, the kind where you're doing chores but there's no urgency so it's not a chore at all, and I gazed down the stairs to the living room. The Morkies (our Maltese-Yorkie pups) were making happy growling sounds as they tackled each other (at twelve pounds each their tumbling was no threat to the furniture), and my husband was humming to himself as he tackled the repair to the kitchen baseboards (chewed the year before by self-same pups when they were teething). Tarps and paintbrushes and dog toys were scattered about and as I surveyed the scene, I remember thinking "What happy chaos" before blissfully wafting down the stairs out the back door.

As I made my way down to the garage I suddenly pitched forward as my foot missed the last step. Fear struck me like a cold shock through my core. Despite my whole body jolting with power to right me, I was only aware of the paving stones rushing up to meet my face and my arm wrenched behind me as I reflexively grabbed for the railing. But my hand couldn't grasp firmly enough, and I could not save myself from falling.

My ankle twisted with an ugly crunch. I remember my husband racing to me, grabbing my arms, then pulling me onto my good leg, and supporting me as I bunny-hopped back up the stairs to the couch. I promptly fainted for about a minute and then came to with a nauseous feeling in my stomach, but relieved to have his care and anti-inflammatories and an ice pack. My whole experience of fear was oriented outward to the source of the danger and how to escape it.

Fast forward a few weeks later and I was at the park across the street with the Morkies when I stepped into a divot in the grass and my still-swollen ankle twisted again. The pain shot up like an electrical current from my ankle to my knee and immediately I was upset with myself. I limped home and over the next few days felt agitated and tense and heard myself saying, "You idiot! What were you thinking? You are so careless. What is the matter with you that you are disconnected from your feet? Twice? Twice you twist your ankle?! And now you probably won't heal well and maybe you've done real damage and what if you can't ski and hike and do all the fun stuff you love? And what if you end up being dependent and need help and then what?"

As I was besieged with those menacing messages, I could feel my muscles bracing and my breath held and my mind racing. I felt threatened and it seemed I needed to *do something* urgently, right now! I was hijacked by anxiety.

Underneath all those stories and criticisms was unrest that had probably been simmering ever since I took the first fall. In fact, I ought to have noticed the unrest sooner, because I had been feeling a bit jumpy and tense and irritable but didn't recognize the call. But now, with the anxiety building and threatening me, I saw what I had been avoiding. My awareness of being a vulnerable human without perfect control over every step and who cannot guarantee she will never fall and sprain her ankle had been tickling at the edges of my awareness. I had been brushing it away with praise for how quickly I had been recuperating.

Once I injured myself again and saw how my journey to wholeness might be longer and more painful than I hoped, the sadness I hadn't wanted to feel about my human limitations refused to be ignored. Instead of being worried about the future and regretful about the past and critical about myself, I blocked those exits from the pain and surrendered.

My sadness rose, and I felt my throat tighten and the weight on my chest felt like an elephant's foot. My shoulders curved forward and my head bowed, and I felt myself let go of the judgment and flow with the sadness. I cried. The waves eventually carried me to compassion, and from there I felt calmer and grew more patient with myself. I was reminded of my limits (darn being human anyway!) and was reunited with the rest of humanity as a flawed yet still worthy being who cannot control things but matters, nonetheless.

So, in the end I obeyed my fear and blocked my anxiety processes and soothed my unrest with warm attention so I could ride waves of emotion to greater authenticity, resilience, and connection. That's how it works!

Waking Up to Reality

I will say it again: this being human gig is not easy. We are so vulnerable. We are embodied sparks of the divine pulled forward by our longing and pushed back by our limits. We need to find a way to get on the path and stay on the path and welcome all the experiences this astounding life has to offer. Yet we are easily distracted by all the shiny objects dancing before us. We need a guidance system to orient us to the precise moments when our heart speaks its truth. And we have one! Unrest arises from our neurobiology that senses emotion as it rises so we can be more authentic, bounce back better from difficulty, open up to closeness, and give our gifts to the world.

Vulnerability is fundamentally human. We cannot *not* feel unrest. And that is absolutely okay. Unrest signals impending truth. You need to be able to notice and respond to that signal, because underneath your unrest is a feeling, one so pure it is like a compass leading you to your deepest self. This wave may carry you gently or propel you violently into heights or depths, but if you ride it out, you will arrive in a new place of calm and clarity, connected to what truly matters and energized to act. Yourself, awake.

The Problem with This Book

Okay, true confession time. I've struggled for years with the problem of this book: how can reading a book help people resolve the conflict between their hunger to grow and their impulse to protect? How can I help people develop an inner sense of themselves when unrest is so unconscious? How can I foster emotional growth through a *book* when I believe deep change arises from *experiences* of unrest and emotion? As a psychologist I have spent decades activating emotion and coregulating unrest in people and holding the experience with them until they can do it for themselves. What I do in my office day after day is so physical and intimate and relational. And here I am offering a book to make a difference...

The biological impulse to avoid unrest cannot be transformed with a few well-chosen words. Old programming to ignore, deny, or catastrophize your bodily experience is not going to simply undo itself based on a taste of cognitive understanding. Nor can willpower be expected to do the job. No amount of reading or thinking or understanding will create a longstanding change in your life. I will not try to sell you the hoax that just *reading* this book will *do* anything at all. I'm sorry to inform you so late in the journey, but there is no quick fix here.

The fact is, we must *do something* if we are to stop the juggernaut of avoidance, numbing, and distraction and awaken to the power of emotion. We need to recognize our old habits and take new steps. Insight is clever and wonderful, but it doesn't *change* things. Understanding helps us choose to take the next step and act but act we must. Insight illuminates the path, but it is our *experience* on the path that transforms us.

Thinking about walking won't get you anywhere; you need to put on your shoes and walk. Unlike cognitive understanding, where you "get it" in one lightning bolt of clarity, emotional growth is a steady, step-by-step process. You must go slowly and repeat it again and again for it to truly take hold, going over the same steps, tracing and retracing until the shift anchors itself in the structures of your brain.

This book isn't about changing your mind. It's about *changing your way of being with yourself* so that when unrest calls, you do what does not come naturally and approach yourself, rather than run away from what you feel. Oops, I forgot, you're just reading a book. You see my dilemma.

Embodying This Book

You are not the unrest. You are not all your exits from unrest. You are not a disembodied head. Nor are you blended into uniformity like some pureed soup. No. You are a shimmering integration of differences, like the sparkling facets that form a diamond or the constantly moving waves and curren· that form the ocean. You are the living relationship between your intelligent and easily wounded body and the clear light of your consciousness shining through. You can recognize unrest and you can hold yourself.

Embodying this book means actively practicing the exercises in each chapter until you begin purposefully to listen for your body's call. It means catching yourself in the moment unrest activates, to unfasten yourself from the automatic habit to brace against your call to growth. Mostly you practice attending to your body, giving language to your sensations. You bring another, larger observing part of yourself to the task, the part of you that loves you as you are, in the place of surrender as you acknowledge your limits, in the painful place of "I can't." As you soothe unrest and allow yourself to be carried by waves of emotion to new shores of yourself, you grow powerful muscles for feeling and being, fully alive.

One of the hardest things about doing this work is how slowly you need to go. The body is slower than the mind and it cannot be rushed. It seems we are all in a chronic rush to the finish line. But you and I will be finished soon enough. And in the meantime, we need to slow ourselves so we can hear and feel and sense what our bodies and hearts and souls need us to know. This is hard for many of us because we have lost the ability to sit still and rest. We live in a world that regards being busy and exhausted as status symbols. We used to gaze into a fire or up at the stars. We used to wait in lineups, listening to our inner thoughts without scanning our social media feed. We used to know how to sit on a bench and watch the breeze as it scattered fallen leaves at our feet. We used to take time to notice if we were tired or hungry or thirsty. And our bodies and hearts and souls still want us to have those experiences.

This reflective observation of inner and outer experience may be familiar to readers who meditate or have a mindfulness or journal practice. Such wonderful applications grow your capacity to focus awareness, which is a very important, even life-altering capacity. But while those practices develop your ability to focus attention in general and perhaps bring compassion to what you find, the awareness work in this book has a specific agenda: attuning you to the precise physical signals of nervous system arousal the moment emotion rises, to direct you toward emotion to foster growth.

I hope to persuade you to act on your own behalf. Don't just get the idea and think it will change your neural wiring.

I invite you to practice being with yourself. Look for the place within that can hold you when unrest calls and *allow yourself to feel yourself being held* as you experience vulnerability. My hope is also scaffolding around you, a supportive structure as you practice having and holding, so that this book becomes a holding around your holding, as you explore this new way of being with yourself.

PRACTICE: DISCERNING UNREST, ANXIETY, AND FEAR

Think of one example each when you have experienced unrest, anxiety, and fear. Then answer three questions about each experience:

1 In the moment, what was the focus of your attention? (Was it danger, thoughts, or sensations heralding vulnerability?)

2 What was the feeling trying to do? (What was the impulse?)

3 What is the takeaway? (What do you understand about the experience now?)

FEAR: Remember that fear is a situation of immediate physical threat, like a large, snarling dog lunging at you, or another driver veering into your lane. Fear is not a thought about a possible future threat or a memory of a past threat. In this exercise you are looking at the fear you felt in the situation at the time. (If you have a trauma history you need to be able to keep a clear awareness that this event is over, in the past, and you have survived. If you feel you are unable to do that, you should skip this exercise until you have the safety and containment that would allow you to look at that historical event without being flooded.)

Think of a situation where you were in danger, perhaps a car accident or a sports accident or a close call of some kind. For example,

"I was skiing down a steep run when I caught an edge and tumbled backward as my ski untethered itself from my bindings and I tumbled down the hill."

1. What was the focus of your attention (the danger)? "I was aware of a rush of adrenaline and the speed of my fall and making sure I didn't hit another skier. I was scrambling to catch hold of something to stop me from falling."

2. What was the feeling trying to do? "The feeling was big energy in my arms and legs as I tried to find something to hold on to, to stop my slide downhill, and also to control myself so I didn't hit anyone else."

3. When you follow the story through to the end, what is the takeaway for you? "I smacked myself pretty hard and was sore for a few days, but I am grateful to my body for having a fast survival reaction and trying its best to save me from being even more hurt."

ANXIETY: Think of a time you were anxious. Remember, this means a time when you had the muscle tension and agitation and other manifestations of nervous system arousal, and you were telling yourself scary or threatening stories of some kind. For example, "I was going to meet my boyfriend's parents for the first time and all I could think about was all the ways I was not what they're looking for in a partner for their son."

1. What was the focus of your attention (the thoughts)? "I was focused self-consciously on my appearance and changed my outfit several times. I worried about what to say to make them like me. I told myself I wasn't good enough. I tortured myself with mental movies of how I will say or do something to embarrass myself."

2. What was the feeling trying to do? "It was distracting me and making me feel tongue-tied and my mind race. This feeling was

telling me I can make them like me, or at least I should be able to. It was giving me the idea that I have control over the outcome."

3 What is the takeaway? "I don't have control over what other people think of me. I felt like they were rejecting me, but my anxiety reveals a rejection of myself that I couldn't see. As a result, I wasn't as present or natural as I wanted to be, and I couldn't relax and be myself."

UNREST: Think of a time when you felt unrest. This means a time when there was a call from your body wanting you to know you were feeling an emotion as it was rising inside you. For example, "I somehow managed to click something on my computer and lost a full day's work. I called my tech guy, and he couldn't get back to me for twenty-four hours and that whole time I was on the edge of my seat not knowing if the work could be found. And when he was able to dig in to help me, he discovered I had accidentally deleted a whole file and it could not be recovered. I was so agitated and so sad."

1 What was the focus of your attention (the sensations heralding vulnerable emotion)? "I was holding my breath and my shoulders were up around my ears. My jaw was clenched, and my mouth was dry, and my stomach felt sick, and I was burping. I was fidgety and couldn't sit still."

2 What was the feeling trying to do? "It was yelling at me to tune in and pay attention inside to help me come to terms with this loss. I was up against a limit to my control over something that mattered to me. I really didn't want to lose eight hours of writing. (And it was good, too. I was on a roll!) But I also didn't want to be cruel to myself, so I paid attention to the bracing and agitation and my body settled."

3 What is the takeaway? "After my body settled, I cried. I cried until the waves passed (it took a while), and at the end I felt

a quiet resolve to start again and just do the best I could. I accepted that my best is all I can do, and I am not a bad person when I make a mistake. I noticed that when I let myself surrender to the sadness, I felt calmer and more confident that, although I might not be able to recreate what I had written, I could produce something else that would be different, but just as good. I bounced back from the setback and didn't beat myself up or collapse into victimhood or have a tantrum. I feel proud of myself."

As you review your examples, note the aspects of your experiences that will help you identify and differentiate unrest from anxiety from fear, so you can recognize these experiences in daily moments in your life. You are already on track, distinguishing these. And that is success!

3

perceiving unrest through your inner senses

---

*"No matter how difficult and painful it may be,
nothing sounds as good to the soul as the truth."*

MARTHA BECK

ET US begin the session by taking a mindful breath into our bodies," said the facilitator. A warm, grey-haired woman with a dancer's body and a lilting laugh, she looked us in the eye, one by one, as we sucked air into our chests. "Only when we are aware of our own reactions can we be responsively aware of others' reactions," she explained.

"Bringing the body into the therapy room" was a revolutionary notion decades ago. Back then, "talk therapy" was the norm for addressing cognitive processes, but this new focus was said to accelerate and deepen the healing work.

A curious graduate student, I had my notepad at the ready but wasn't buying into the physical stuff. As the workshop continued, the facilitator invited us to check in and notice our bodily sensations and to deliberately *feel* what we felt. Though I liked her manner, I couldn't help feeling irked with her slow process. My impatient brain snapped its fingers and tapped its feet, muttering, "Okay, okay, I've got this, let's move along!" The concepts were obvious to my rational, cognitive self, so I couldn't understand why we were taking so long with them. "Let's get to the actual material, not focus on our gurgling stomachs and aching necks."

I looked around the room and thought the other participants seemed much kinder people than me. They appeared to be doing as instructed, while I was thinking that the ideas mattered, not this experiential fluff. I shrugged it off and took my notes and felt a bit superior. I was blind to how avoidance of the slow-felt experience of my own body foretold my fall . . .

Paying Attention to Your Internal Sensations

Interoception is the process of perceiving and paying attention to your internal sensations. It is like a sense organ for your inner self. Your nervous system senses and interprets signals from your body in a moment-to-moment flow. When you know you are hungry or thirsty or tired or cold, you are using your interoceptive ability to notice your inner state. You know how fast or hard your heart is beating, how dry your mouth is, how tense your muscles are, whether your stomach is upset or you're holding your breath. You can know lots more than that about yourself and are meant to. You are meant to "bring the body" into your whole life.

Unrest is not a comfortable feeling, nor is it meant to be. Unrest is a spike because it is *meant* to grab you. It tells you something crucial is happening, right now! When emotional growth knocks at your door, you are activated, and your body asks if this is a physical threat: "Am I safe?" Unless there is an immediate threat to life and limb—and there rarely is—you need to answer in the affirmative and pay warm interest to your bracing and agitation. But often unrest is below your awareness, so you need to train yourself to be open to it, or you'll miss its transformational call.

Unrest lets you in on the most wonderful thing: your point of contact with vulnerability. The abstract, abiding fact that you are vulnerable becomes an immediate, physical experience of *being vulnerable*, opening you to an opportunity for growth, here, right now. Your interoceptive ability allows you to notice and care for unrest so you can pierce the veil of unconsciousness and open to your rich inner complexity. For example, you see a person living on the street, and you notice your shoulders hunched around your ears and, instead of assuming you're afraid of that person and creating some story about why they might be a threat, you get curious. "Hmm, something is up... Yes, my shoulders are up! And my breathing is shallow, and my hands are fidgety. Something is up inside of me, something that needs my attention right now. I'm going to give my shoulders and breath and hands my undivided attention right in this moment and see what happens." As you attune to those sensations, your body senses your presence and lets go a little. When it does, you are more grounded and connected to yourself, and you become aware of some feeling that you almost overlooked. You may feel anger about the injustice of a system that leaves people to fend for themselves with so little support or sadness about the magnitude of the problem or compassion toward the person on the street or gratitude for your blessings of shelter and food. You may be moved to act, even if to simply make gentle

eye contact. And in that experience, you come to know yourself more deeply.

You are supposed to feel unrest. It is not a weakness or
a problem to be solved. Hunger and thirst and fatigue and
bladder pressure are physical signals asking you to do something—eat, drink, rest, or urinate. Those signals aren't
comfortable or pleasant, but we don't complain about them
as though they are a problem that should go away. Without
them, you might neglect yourself until you starve or dehy-
drate or faint from exhaustion or just pee your pants. Like
those important cues, unrest also asks you to do something—
to tune in and pay attention. It beseeches you to notice nervous
system arousal, to pay attention and soothe it, so you can
access emotion and grow.

The Hardest and Greatest Gift I Ever Received

I understand the resistance to being in the body better than
you might think. I always had huge emotional experiences
and humongous ideas. I was an intense kid, carried fast and
hard by life's ups and downs. I reacted strongly to events and
people, and I tracked others like a bird dog. I swooned at the
smell of freshly cut grass and wept at the death of a grasshop-
per. I regularly wanted to kill my little sister (who is now my
dearest friend). I held my breath and braced when my mother
anxiously awaited the bill for our groceries at the supermarket
checkout. But I did not register how those experiences were
resonating, like a song of myself, in my body.

My childhood roller coaster was invisible to my mother in
her busy and difficult life, raising four daughters on her own. I
am deeply grateful and in awe of how she managed to protect
and provide for us, but she had little emotional capacity for
my sisters and me. So, I adapted to the emotional neglect by

learning to neglect myself. I learned to ignore my inner self, and for my first three decades was powered via twin forces of will and impulse. Once I set my mind to my heart's agenda, I could ignore discomfort and push through without regard. That might sound pretty good, but there was a cost. I was sorrowfully out of touch with unrest in my body, so I did not recognize the limits to control over things that mattered to me. I either "made it happen" through sheer will, or I didn't see it *not happening* because I looked the other way, or I lied to myself that I "didn't really want it anyway."

Still, I was blessed with enough gifts to follow my dreams and persist in the face of challenge for a long time. After my second year of university, I took off for London, England, to live and work for a few years. On that adventure, I met and married my husband and helped him immigrate to Canada. As he retrained in naturopathic medicine, I went back to university, waitressing full time to support us both. I was the first person in my family to complete an undergraduate degree. I worked hard and received scholarships into a master's program and then a PhD program in clinical psychology. But even as I trained to help others resolve their emotional difficulties, I was woefully out of touch with the truth of my life.

I was nearing the end of my PhD when the guts of my life were ripped open. After twelve years of marriage and my financial and emotional support, my husband admitted he had been cheating with his receptionist for three years. He only came clean when his mistress threatened to introduce me to their six-month-old baby.

And the walls to my body crumbled. A river of truth poured in, rushing in torrents through my arms and legs and bloodstream, washing away the barriers to my conscious knowing of what my body already knew. Waves of grief and anger and pain carried me so far from the shore of my old life that I lost all my familiar bearings. My helper identity dissolved, and I realized I needed my own help immediately. All the secrets I had held from myself pierced through the veil, and I witnessed my self-neglect. I saw the part I had played in this awful drama.

Over the years I had ignored his subtle disdain and overlooked his selfishness. I didn't acknowledge it, even to myself. Or if I did, my mind had a story for it. He'd come from a rather advantaged social background, so I told myself his entitlement was a vestige of that class privilege, and he didn't really *mean* anything by it. Or I made his insensitive remarks a cute idiosyncrasy, as English was not his first language. Or I thought it too trivial to address: "It's not a big deal." Or I told myself, "He didn't really mean it." I minimized and I over-functioned. I busied myself and I ignored signs of stress. I pushed myself, and I distracted myself, and I made up stories about how things were. And my untrained heart wanted so much to believe my lies.

About two months before his confession, I was alone in the house on the stairs up to the bedroom and I saw and felt someone up close facing me, and I saw and felt them stick me in the ribs with a shiv. I doubled over and had to grab the bannister to hold myself up. The hallucination took my breath away. It was so real. I remember having the thought that to stab someone from behind was easy, even a stranger could do it. But to stab someone from the front, up close and personal, a person had to be intimate. And then... wait for it... *I just shrugged it off.*

Ignoring myself was not easy. I had to suppress my body's dispatches: a certain hollowness inside, little quivers of uncertainty as I looked in his eyes, a held breath as I came in the door and wondered how I'd be greeted. "Don't be silly," I chided myself and counted my blessings. I silenced my body with lots of study and work and food. Over that three-year period of the affair "of which I knew nothing," I gained almost forty pounds as I shut up, shut down, and shut off my body. I had "no idea" what was prompting me to soothe myself with food every night. I just felt shame and blame and not good enough. And I smiled bravely through, a soldier in the stoic army.

When his mistress threatened to reveal my husband's secret to me, he came to me expecting I would make it all okay as I had always done. He believed that nothing would change. "It's not like I love her or anything," he said, "and I think you will like the baby."

But the truth ripped through me, and everything changed. It was the hardest and greatest gift I have ever received. Nauseous frozen shock made my legs give way as I fell to my knees on the soft grey carpet in the living room. I surrendered to the truth as pulsating waves of anger and grief crested and ebbed, again and again. I raged and I wept, and I came alive in my ragged breathing and my pounding heart. Blood began to surge into my legs to help me make my stand. A fiery force rose in my chest, and I found my voice. I mattered, finally, in my matter.

I told him he had to leave. And after being so lonely for so long in my fog of denial with him, I discovered being alone is not lonely when you are present with yourself.

Over several months he tried to woo me back. His pleading eyes and soft cooing tones still stirred the place in my heart where I had loved him, but much stronger was the physical truth of my emotions. It took courage, but day after day I leaned toward my body and said "bring it on" as the waves washed me clean to my core. I felt my very cellular structure was transforming as I came home to myself in my body. The weight I had gained over three years fell off like unneeded armor, revealing my soft strength, my loving connection with myself.

Had I been connected in my body like this so many years before, I'd never have married him. His detachment, self-absorption, and casual lack of empathy would have felt like violations. I would have known something was not right, and I would have mattered enough to move along. Had I been raised where emotion was prized and regulated, I would have known to tune in to my feelings. I would have trusted what goes up will come down and comforted myself with the thought that when it does, I will find myself in a good place. I would have been confident I could manage the pain of the truth because I had soothed painful feelings so many times before. I would have risked knowing what was wrong and could never be made right in my marriage and been able to choose to leave long before.

Whispers from the Body

Out of this profound personal transformation arose a tectonic shift in my work with clients. I came to see how noticing and experiencing unrest in the body can accelerate emotional maturation. Yes, catastrophic things can open us to feel and grow, but so too can small things, if felt deeply. My ticklish delight as a little girl mesmerized by a ladybug tottering on the back of my hand is as good an entry point to my vulnerability as any car crash. I am moved. We all are moved. And when we allow ourselves to recognize the precise moment of that stirring, we can come home to the body, soothe its signal of unrest, feel deeply, and grow.

In my sessions with clients, I began to slow down and track the body moment to moment. It was almost like having two new people in the therapy room, my body and that of my client, whose body needed to be listened to with the same exquisite precision as their words. Small shifts and contractions and sighs were sharing a whole other level of information and truth, arguably even more important than the story being told with language. Like the whisperings from my own body, my physiology resonated with my clients as they revealed themselves, enriching my empathy and understanding of their experience.

This urge to avoid the whisperings of your body is part of your human legacy. Your soul's hunger to experience every tingle of life through your senses is curbed by your body's mission to keep you alive, and the tension between those forces provides the best opportunity for you to emerge into all you are deeply meant to be. But for many of us, the balance has become too conservative, and now we misread mere vulnerability as danger. Our brains habitually tune out the flow of experience from our bodies. We use the bare minimum of sensory information to jump to conclusions about the present based on the past. We are not experiencing here and now. So, although your thinking brain might want to rush through this book looking for ideas, I ask you to give your feeling, experiencing brain time to catch up. Your *idea* of connecting to the body and the *felt sense* of your connection are as different from one another as a clinical description of sex is from the intimate, multisensory, embodied experience of making love with someone you care for deeply. You really have to be there.

The simple heart of this book is this: the way you pay attention to sensations of unrest is the foundation for growth. When you deliberately detect and feel your bodily arousal, you calm your body and open yourself to the flow of emotion that will mature you. Interoception is your sense organ that lets you tune in to yourself. Your interoceptive senses discern your inner state. And you can improve them with practice.

I'm making a big deal about a small thing. Unrest is a tiny biological cue that people habitually tune out. It seems almost too puny to notice. In early sessions, patients inevitably look at me like I have two heads when I invite them to pay attention to physical signals of unrest. What on earth could be important about their tapping foot or fidgety hands or held breath? "I always do that," they say. "It doesn't mean a thing."

We avoid experiencing life and we ignore unrest at great cost to ourselves and to the planet. For something as easy to overlook as tense shoulders or a chewed lip, unrest is a small signal that, if unheeded, ejects us from the power of the living moment.

Paralyzed by Panic

I live in Vancouver, British Columbia, a beautiful green place nestled against the mountains on the Pacific Ocean, with many inlets and crossings and a big river called the Fraser. The city is "panic exposure central." On a bridge there is no exit; you cannot escape so you must commit and keep going. Simply getting to my office involves crossing one or two or even three bridges for some clients.

Barb was convinced she would panic on the bridge and forget how to drive. She routinely pictured herself driving off the bridge or into the oncoming lane. She found all sorts of ways to distract herself from what she was feeling as she drove over the Granville or Cambie or Burrard or Lion's Gate bridge. She'd roll her windows up and down, count backward from one hundred by sevens, imagine being on a beach in Mexico, or bring along her magic amulets (a water bottle, a packet of gum, and a bottle of medication that she didn't use but just "felt safer" having along). She was so happy when she could report to me that she'd felt nothing as she crossed the bridge, as though that were a success. Unfortunately for her, not feeling uncomfortable sensations meant she might as well have refrained from the exercise, since feeling the discomfort *was* the treatment.

A panic attack is an unpleasant experience—and anyone who has had one knows that is a huge understatement. A heavy weight of impending doom descends upon the body as a shot of adrenaline fires into the bloodstream and the heart begins to pound and race. Muscles tense and clench and ready themselves for action. A cascade of dizziness, faintness, tingling, hot flushes and cold chills, and a feeling of suffocation accompany the shallow breathing of hyper-ventilation. Overwhelming terror drives people to conclude falsely that what's happening is a catastrophe. They fear they will lose control of themselves and think they need to "do something" to avoid humiliation or worse. These stories are often connected to places where escape is impossible or would be embarrassing, like elevators and airplanes or quiet bank lineups. Those conclusions almost always worsen the problem.

For many years, several times a year, I ran a ten-week group program for people struggling with panic disorder. Originally guided by cognitive-behavioral principles of chal-lenging misconceptions and practicing exposure to feared activities and situations, I found myself working more and more with the bodily sensations of those intelligent, moti-vated folks who were paralyzed by panic. My work with them emboldened me to prioritize tuning in to sensations in the body. My gratitude to them is immense.

For Barb and many people with panic disorder, the only way to function is to push through while gritting their teeth and ignoring their feelings. But too many people begin their journey with panic by avoiding here and there, only to find eventually they are living a smaller and smaller life. They get out there and get the job done but never truly face their fears, so they never resolve their panic problem. The thing they *think* they fear, like sitting in a movie theater or flying in an airplane, is not the real source of their dread. What people really fear is the *physical feelings* in their bodies. But since they don't perceive the real trigger for their impulse to run away, they make sense of themselves by conjuring stories.

Humans are meaning-making creatures; we need to understand ourselves. People who panic explain their reactions by citing plane crash statistics and elevator safety records and the cruel judgments of others. Those scary stories transform unpleasant sensations into hellish experiences. Folks panic themselves with tales of facing (or narrowly escaping) some unbearably dangerous or embarrassing catastrophe. Despite their compelling disaster stories, the truth is their bodies are suddenly agitated and tense and shaky, powered up to run or fight. And they don't want to feel that way.

Barb and I worked hard to dig into her bodily experience of panic. I invited her to vividly imagine herself in her car heading onto the bridge. Her impulse to resist feeling was massive, but we persisted until she could let herself fully experience the sensations. She felt her sweaty palms and her shaky legs. She thought those sensations meant she'd lose control of the steering wheel and her ability to hit the brakes. "Just a story," I murmured, and asked her to stay with it. "Keep feeling your body right now." She began to shake and shed some tears.

We focused on her body until, after what felt like forever for Barb but was about three minutes, she began to feel better. The practice in the office was followed up with more practice in the car, and after several weeks of actively tuning in and perceiving her internal state while driving over a bridge, she gleefully declared herself panic-free.

X-ray Vision Superpower

Barb developed interoception, the most remarkable super-power. Paying attention to sensations in trigger situations empowered her to stay with herself with compassion, and she began to confront all sorts of situations she'd been avoiding. Her life became bigger and freer than she'd ever dreamed.

Interoception is a superpower because it gives you X-ray vision into deeper levels of yourself. It is your window to unconscious signaling, so you can tune in and take care of yourself sooner and make the most of your opportunities for growth. We vary in our innate interoceptive ability, but with practice we can all improve at noticing what we feel inside.

The impulse to avoid or escape the body became apparent to me when I worked with people suffering from panic disorder. I became expert at helping them go past their stories and movies to the thing underneath... the uncomfortable sensations themselves. "Fear of fear" is at the root of panic disorder. But it is also at the root of what's going on for *us all* when unrest stirs! It is simply the human condition. We are all wired to move away from the discomfort of unrest. My wonderful panic patients revealed to me the massive growth-promoting power of interoception: precisely noticing small sensations and calming them with warm interest.

People are invariably surprised at the reception they get when they come home to the body and pay close attention to sensations. Often, they have tried many strategies to get rid of anxiety, with limited success. They have tried to talk themselves out of it, meditate themselves above it, distract themselves away from it, and push themselves through it,

"No one can listen to your body for you. To grow and heal you have to take responsibility for listening to it yourself."

JON KABAT-ZINN

all with the agenda of stopping this discomfort. They have tried to silence it and escape it. But whatever they have done typically does not work in the long run, and they remain agitated, tense, and restless.

Interoception allows you to notice and soothe unrest from the inside so that you can act early, rather than ignoring yourself until you are faced with anxiety, impulsivity, or numbing and depression. This small awareness is a massive thing because it gives you conscious access to the moment when growth is most available.

But it does more than that. When you pay careful, compassionate attention to sensations of unrest, you are welcomed home with a release in tension. Your unrest is soothed. Your body allows itself to relax and luxuriate in the world around it.

How could something so simple as awareness change the state of your body? Why does your body let go when you tune in? The answer is in the remarkable survival imperative wired into your nervous system.

Growth versus Survival

The body teaches us a vital lesson about growth and survival: they are opposites. When you are safe, you can devote your energy inward, to healing and growth. Every day your body loses trillions of cells, and when you are safe, blood is directed to your internal organs, where immune function and cell reproduction can repair and replace them. When you are safe, your body sends blood to your forebrain, where reflective processes allow you to relax, be creative, laugh, and think in deeper and more complex ways.

But when you are in danger, the body goes into survival mode and orients outward, with all systems functioning to fight or flee. Blood goes to the extremities and away from the core, and cellular turnover halts. Your thinking becomes black and white, shallow, and eventually, if the threat is too high, goes offline completely.

The body prioritizes survival. It's a no-brainer: growth is optional if your survival is on the line. But protection takes energy. *The more protection you require for survival the less energy is available for growth.* Living in a chronic state of survival depletes your resources and prevents growth and healing. You squander energy to defend yourself against your feelings. You deprive yourself of the vitalizing energy that comes from feeling your healthy emotions.

Imagine if an air-raid siren sent a whole region into an underground shelter for survival. The residents could last there for a while, but if no one ever told them the danger had passed, they would run out of supplies, their farms would be left untended, and there would be no food or industry or education or culture... All development and growth would cease. And eventually the people would die. We are not meant to stay in survival mode forever. We are meant to exit the shelter and grow in the sunlight.

When you live as though your feelings are threats, you are enduring life, not fully living. You are oriented outward like a frightened prey animal, disconnected from your truth—the unique meaning of your experience, for you. You are a singular channel for experiences of being alive. Your longings and memories and DNA and current state and physiology shape how what happens to you informs and energizes you. Your eyes perceive shapes and color, as do mine. And yet, what I see is not identical to what you see, since my cornea, iris, lens, and visual cortex process the waves of light in ways that differ from yours. We both listen to the same music, but what I hear is precisely attuned to qualities in my tympanic membrane and cochlea and my auditory cortex, and what you hear is a result of yours. As you touch the world and the world touches you, everything is funneled through the conduit of your soul's hunger for life and your physical being. You are the only you, and you matter in all the distinctive ways you experience your life.

Survival has kept you alive, and now it is time for you to grow. Growth involves experiencing, connecting, opening, approaching, and exploring with curiosity.

The deal in emotional survival is "don't feel and you don't die." The deal in emotional growth is "feel and be fully alive." But this is so much harder to do than it looks because unrest feels like something you ought to avoid. The very moment you are confronted with the reality of your limits to control over something that matters to you, your body tenses. Perhaps you have reservations at a restaurant and are waiting for your husband to come home, and he is late, and you see his cell phone charging in the kitchen. Right away your back stiffens and your heart rate speeds up, and you can feel a surge of adrenaline coursing through your bloodstream. You feel agitated and it feels like nervousness, like something is "wrong." At an unconscious level it seems like there is a threat or danger. But there is no danger at all. There may be some annoyance because he often forgets his phone, and it is time to sit down and have a good heart-to-heart conversation about what it feels like for you when he doesn't make sure he can be reached. But if you do not soothe the unrest and assure your body there is no danger, you may rely on old habits to deny what you feel, distracting yourself in the moment with fantasies of being a bigger person than you are, but then later find yourself having one too many glasses of wine at the restaurant. We often unconsciously disconnect from ourselves when unrest stirs. Most of us are gone before we even knew there was a signal.

When you are in real danger, fear mobilizes you to deal with the external threat. If an out-of-control truck is speeding toward you, your senses scan to calculate the speed and direction of the hurtling vehicle and to see where you might be able to leap to avoid being hit. You are incapable of drawing attention inward in that moment. Your glutes and quads are firing, your lungs are brimming with air, and your heart is racing. Blood is also redirected from the forebrain to the hindbrain, where your more primitive survival centers are located. Your thinking becomes simple. You are commanded and energized to protectively avoid or escape.

This is as it needs to be. In survival, you do what you need to do to stay alive. In that moment you *cannot* tune in to and experience those sensations inside your body, even if I offer you a hundred thousand dollars to do so.

Cindy was going about her daily work as a bank teller when a man pointed a gun at her and told her to fill a bag with cash from her till, or else. When we discussed her trauma in our first session, she said she had no physical awareness of herself at the time of the robbery. In fact, when the police arrived, she had no memory of what she had felt at all during the event. Her interoception was offline. But she was acutely aware of important details about the source of the danger, which to the chagrin of the investigators did not include the face or dress of the perpetrator. Instead, she gave them an exquisitely vivid description of the gun, the shiny grey metal of its dark barrel aiming at her.

Only much later, *when she was safe enough* to begin processing what had happened, could Cindy connect with what had been going on inside her. She could register how terrified she'd been, robotlike as she handed over the bag of money. She could feel the icy fear in her veins and hear the loud pounding of her heart and the wobbly jelly feeling in her legs. And as she felt all this in safety with me, she also remembered the movie of her own death that had played while he had the gun to her; she had seen herself shot and bleeding, slumped against the wall, her last thoughts being how much she loved her mother. Only once her body was out of the traumatized state and no longer felt she was in danger could she experience her rage and helplessness and grief. In facing all her feelings, she could finish the trauma and feel in her body that it was all over now.

When you actively pay attention to your sensations in the here and now, you tell your body that it is safe. Your precise inner attention lets your body know that the sensation that triggered your nervous system is *not danger*. You must *do something* to let your body know it is safe. Interoception is that thing.

But Vulnerability Is Weakness!

When Katya first came in to see me, she was devastated, at the grim end of her long marriage. Warm, kind, and a wonderful mother, Katya had an elegance that shone through her awful lack of self-worth. Her husband had been a serial philanderer, and she had blamed herself for his neglect for years. At the discovery of his third affair, Katya drew the line and insisted her husband either seek counseling with her or leave.

To her dismay, he chose to leave. She felt utterly rejected. She beat herself up going over all the ways she should have done things differently, how she should have been stronger and slimmer and more cheerful and more patient. Katya held herself to a standard that would have tested a saint. From our very first visit it was clear that, long before her husband rejected her, she had rejected herself.

Katya felt she had to be perfect, which meant she should not be affected by the ups and downs of big emotion. She never slowed down. She took care of everyone and everything, except herself. She felt ashamed when she was too tired to finish the yardwork or couldn't figure out how to fix the washer or even when she fell ill. Once she was so sick with food poisoning that she was unable to get to the bathroom and projectile vomited, and even though she herself cleaned everything up, all she could say for days was "sorry, sorry, sorry." When people or situations disappointed her, she tried to look on the bright side; when someone talked over her or kept her waiting, she kept a lid on her anger. If life did not go smoothly, she made it look as though it had. She didn't want to accept that sometimes we all have problems. If she could control things and herself and the world, then she would feel better.

But Katya rarely felt better. She usually felt not good enough. She had set the bar so high that the reality of being a vulnerable human was unacceptable. She found it difficult to see that her husband's behavior reflected on him and not her. That would mean she was too helpless, and Katya would rather believe that she could have done something differently than accept that she had no ultimate say in how he behaved. Katya feared what that vulnerable truth would feel like and saw it as too weak and horrible and hopeless to bear.

Crying Over Spilled Milk

Your human heart is a tender thing. You can be affected, moved, hurt. You undoubtedly have been, many times. Life is full of uncertainty, unpredictability, and loss. Forces outside you decide how all sorts of things that matter to you turn out. This is true, of course, of all living things. But humans are a special case. We have the remarkable capacity to reflect on our experiences. We can *know* we are vulnerable. We can be aware of the gap between what we want and what we can make happen.

And this gap is not just a concept, it *feels* like something: your diaphragm tightening, your quads tensing, your neck bracing, your hands fidgeting. Unrest matters *in your matter*, and it needs to matter to you. But unrest also happens fast and can be subtle and you have probably learned to ignore it. You move away from discomfort unconsciously. You are online shopping or munching on food you were not even hungry for, or you are checking your social media feed and you didn't even register the quiver in your biceps and your tapping toes. You are ejected from your inner world so quickly you don't notice you're gone.

But sometimes you are aware of unrest and argue with reality. You reflexively dread the truth of your vulnerability, so you reject your limited control over what you desire. You get mad at yourself, or you get mad at the world. You tell yourself you should be able to make "it" happen and if it isn't working out the way you want, then you are weak or a failure. Or you might shake your fist at the world and get caught in bitter stories of unfairness.

I was in a big rush the other morning. As is often the way when we ignore unrest and override our limits, I didn't give myself enough time. And I caused myself to take even more time! Reaching to pour milk into my teacup, I knocked the carton and it tipped off the end of the counter, splattering milk all over the kitchen floor. As the white liquid fanned out over the dark granite, adrenaline washed through my bloodstream. I was now going to be even later than I'd predicted and another task would have to drop off the list. Yet understanding how experience avoidance leads to suffering, I felt compelled to slow down to feel my unrest.

What an extraordinarily difficult thing to do! The impulse to speed up and ignore my feelings was strong. But I took my own advice and slowed down and noticed the tight muscles in my hands and shoulders, my braced diaphragm, and my suspended breath. I went even slower and asked myself to *feel* what I had noticed. I felt the fidgetiness and the tension and the tightness and stayed with it until I noticed a slight release. I took a few mindful breaths and looked at the spilled milk and allowed myself to matter. I was amazed to find I could do that *and* wipe up the milk!

Instead of cursing myself with "Oh, *#%!, you clumsy oaf," instead of being annoyed and critical of myself, instead of simply enduring and clenching and being "not there" for myself, I refrained from adding one bit more to what was already hard enough. I was already stressed. My body was on alert and trying to do its best for me, unsure if we were in danger. I chose to hear that message and respond by slowing down and caring about how I felt. I felt the discomfort and stayed with it.

And wonder of wonders, taking the extra ten seconds or thirty seconds, or even two minutes didn't throw off my day's schedule! But it did change the energy of my day. It changed my energy. It made me feel valued. Rather than being irritated with myself or projecting irritation onto the world or disconnecting from myself, and potentially from others, I stayed and comforted myself. I demonstrated that I matter. Even then. Perhaps sometimes we do need to cry over, or at least care about, spilled milk.

Unrest lets us know we have a choice, right in this instant, to come home and comfort ourselves in moments of vulnerability. But to benefit from unrest's benevolent invitation, we need to go slowly and tune in carefully.

The Heart of Being Human

In our work together, Katya began to see how she neglected herself when vulnerable, how quickly she left herself when life struck a limit. I coached her to notice her body in the moment. Her first efforts were peppered with remarks like "I shouldn't feel this way," "This seems indulgent," and "This really isn't a big deal." I just kept asking her to tune in to her sensations of unrest as she shared her daily challenges with supporting her kids, handling her job, and managing her separation.

Little by little, Katya's ability to notice her body improved and, although it still felt indulgent, she became quite good at noticing when her muscles began to tense and her breathing sped up. Then we'd always slow down a bit more and see if she could stay with it long enough to sense a shift as her body registered her warm interest and the unrest began to settle. Katya's delight at her success was contagious. With each cycle of perceiving unrest and responding effectively, she became more confident. "I can feel bad and nothing bad happens. In fact, I can make the feeling bad feel better!"

The careful work took many months, but it brought Katya to a place of seeing her own feelings as valuable and important. With support, she let herself tell the truth of what it had felt like to be treated dismissively for so many years. She accessed and tolerated her anger and her grief. Rather than turn away from her pain, she turned toward it and felt her own care. She surprised herself: "I would never in the past have even stopped to think about what I feel, much less let myself stay with it and feel it."

Yet feel it she did, and as she did, she connected to an old memory of being a small child with her cold immigrant mother whose terrible unresolved losses drove her to feel nothing was ever good enough. Katya could never fix her mother's losses, but she sure tried. She realized that her rejection of her own limits in her marriage was really a solution to an old problem from long ago. Believing she could and should somehow *make* her mother happy, she didn't have to feel the pain of her helplessness to win her mother's approval or love. As a child, Katya had wrapped herself in the fantasy that she took care of her mother: "I protected my mother from my needs and my distress." If the problem was within her, maybe she could fix it... if it was outside her, she was helpless. And the truth of her helplessness felt unbearable.

As Katya accepted herself in her limits, she emerged with vivacious joie de vivre that had been hiding all along under her need to be perfect. She could better connect with people and made many new friends. She found herself taking risks and trying new things that would have felt too vulnerable before.

"My fear of feeling, especially of feeling vulnerable, stopped me from being me," she reflected in one of our last sessions. "I missed so much of my life. I am so much better now, but I still have some holding on and second-guessing. But I can have doubts without negating my strength. I can feel sad and vulnerable and angry. I am a lot more passionate than I realized."

Those who argue that feeling our vulnerability means being open, exposed, defenseless, and helpless are right. But, paradoxically, all this is strength. When we are faced with limits to control over outcomes that matter to us, and can embrace the truth of that, we are more powerful and healthy.

PRACTICE: INTEROCEPTION—LEARNING TO LISTEN IN

Over the next few days, see if you can catch yourself as you are hungry or thirsty or tired or feel cold. Perhaps you will not immediately catch the body's signal, but you may notice yourself reach for a bite to eat or a glass of water or notice yourself doze off or grab a sweater. See if you can tell *how* you know what you need. What specific cues guide you to grab a snack or pull a sweater over your shoulders? Be as precise as you can. Don't just skim over with a global statement: "I'm tired." What exactly does tired feel like in your body? In your neck and shoulders and stomach and arms and face and legs...

After practicing with these more familiar signals for a few days, begin to look for unrest. Keep an eye open for situations of vulnerability: maybe you are running late for an appointment, waiting on test results, looking forward to seeing an old friend you haven't seen in years, or your cat just barfed on your carpet. Tune in to yourself and look for muscle tension. Check your shoulders and hands and notice if you are holding your breath. You can also easily check your pulse rate using just your fingers either at the wrist or at the side of the neck. At the wrist, lightly press the index and middle fingers of one hand on the opposite wrist, just below the base of the thumb. Or lightly press the side of the neck just below your jawbone. Count the number of beats in fifteen seconds and multiply by four to obtain your heart rate. You can also use a smart watch if you have one, or a pulse oximeter, a small device you can buy for around seventy dollars and clip onto your fingertip. This kind of rapid biofeedback can show you how simply thinking about something vulnerable triggers physiological changes. As you practice tuning in and reading your pulse rate, you can get better at feeling how fast your heart is beating and improve your ability to bring it down by paying inner attention. When you notice these signals, say hello as though you are happy to greet them. You are now listening in, and that is success!

The Roots of Avoidance:
Three Obstacles to Perceiving Unrest

At least three deep roots feed our reflex to avoid unrest: our neural wiring, our developmental history, and our feeling-phobic culture.

Neural Wiring

As we have discussed, the impulse to avoid discomfort is normal. You are wired from birth with basic brain mechanisms that draw you toward what feels good and away from what feels bad. For example, if you put lemon juice on an infant's tongue, she will grimace and stick her tongue out. If you surprise her with a loud noise, she will cry. The infant doesn't have to learn those reactions.

So, without any outside influence, without any learning or social pressure, you are already set up from your earliest days to move away from experiences that feel uncomfortable. And unrest is uncomfortable. Even more, built into the discomfort of unrest itself is a signal that feels like threat. It is just how our nervous system works. The circuitry that tells us we are on the cusp of a vulnerable emotional experience is the exact same one that says we are about to be eaten. That unrest and fear share this same neural pathway is a huge deal. Everything you do to approach and feel unrest runs against this grain. You cannot help but feel a sense of threat and yet you must still lean toward the source of that feeling. You see how brave you are?

Developmental Experiences

Many of us have been shaped by childhood experiences to expect pain if we let ourselves feel vulnerable. In chapter five, we will explore in detail how being left alone in our felt sense of vulnerability when we were small molded adult-brain pathways that lead us away from ourselves when unrest calls.

Feeling-Phobic Culture

There is an underlying lie in our culture that hard things grow us. We are told to toughen up and that we are stronger in the broken places. But that depends on your definition of strength. While a bone mends stronger after breaking, that is a temporary effect, an interim scaffold of calcium to bridge the injury. If it breaks again in the same spot, it may heal more slowly. Think of scar tissue—what it gains in toughness it loses in flexibility and sensitivity.

We tend to admire those who endure without complaint. And in our "can-do, take charge" culture, emotion is far too yielding an experience to admire. Doing is active, whereas feeling is something that *happens* to you. We do not want to be acted upon, affected, moved without our say-so.

Our hard-bellied cultural bracing presses against our soft heart that wants to feel. But we are not meant to simply endure this life. The problem with enduring is that someone gets forgotten. While you are busy not noticing what you feel, some part of you *is* feeling. While you are being bigger than what is happening to you, someone within is little and afraid and hurting. Meanwhile, so pleased with yourself that your rapidly beating heart does not even register to you, that very organ, so wise and knowing, is ignored and neglected, just as you were when you were little. And yes, you do survive, but survival is not growth.

The kernel of truth in the notion that hard things mature us is this: if you embrace unrest and feel the pain of emotion, so blossoms authenticity, resilience, and connections with others. It is not toughening against your tender heart but *experiencing* the hard things *with compassion* that grows you. As you open to what does not feel good and allow it to matter, you can matter. Then everything else can matter, too.

We are torn. We need to show up for this brilliant, brief life we are given, tune in to our pangs of unrest, and risk feeling as deeply as we can bear. Yet we are wired to move away from what does not feel good (and unrest for sure does not feel good), and society obliges with more exits than we could ever use in ten lifetimes. We cannot blame society for this. It's time to wake up and choose.

We swim in waters that say our strength resides in not feeling vulnerability. There is an expression: if you ask a fish about water, he answers, "What water?" Can you see the water you are swimming in? Do you feel how you are pulled away from the moment into the future and past with tricks and distractions? The chronic busyness, the social media competitions, the frantic exercising, the blue light of your iPad in bed with you at night, the drugs, the drinks, the food, the compelling lie that you can have it all ... Can you hear the falsehood of "it doesn't matter"? Can you catch the message of "there's no point indulging feelings"? Can you, compassionately and patiently, dig into where you are tempted to abandon yourself and follow the trail of bodily breadcrumbs back home to your heart?

Regulated Emotion Is Never "Too Much"

Many of us on occasion have felt flooded by our feelings. We may have erupted in ways we regret or collapsed with the weight of the floodwaters. Some of us have been around folks whose emotional experience was out of control. Seeing someone overwhelmed feels awful, as does being overwhelmed ourselves. And the story we tell is that big emotions, especially anger and sadness, are bad things. We think they are harmful, weak, and that they can even make us sick.

Yet the missing piece in this story is invisible unrest. When you notice unrest and pay precise and careful attention, your body settles, and emotion flows smoothly. If you don't notice unrest, you can't soothe it. Unregulated unrest ramps up your emotion and distorts it, adding urgency and pressure. The unrest and emotion become entangled and overwhelming. You experience a warped version of your emotion that leaves you feeling explosive or dysfunctional or depleted.

When emotional experience feels "too much," that is overwhelm. The fault lies not in the emotion itself but in the mixture of emotion and unregulated unrest. Unfortunately, because unrest has always been an invisible force, we have not understood its role in creating upheaval and despair. For example, you may have read that anger can make you ill, yet when you look closer, you may see that the explosive eruption or chronic suppression of anger is what's bad for the body, creating hypertension and inflammation. Similarly, some research shows elevated inflammation among bereaved people, increasing their risk of illness and death. However, at closer inspection we learn how those folks with higher inflammation are "pining for the deceased," have a sense that life is meaningless now that their loved one is gone, and are unable to accept the reality of the loss. In other words, they are not yet *feeling* the grief but instead are overwhelmed with an unregulated mix of unrest and emotion. They avoid their pain through defenses of denial and hopelessness.

Interoceptive blindness and unresolved conflict between the truth of emotion and the lies of defenses are what make people sick. Emotion, free of unregulated unrest, is always healthy and adaptive. Dysfunction, overreactions, shutdown, aggression, depression, and symptoms of physical illness are all caused by unrecognized and unsoothed unrest.

Emotion is the gold, but the discomfort of unrest is your starting point, and interoception is the alchemy that transforms what doesn't feel good into feeling fully alive.

4

harnessing
vulnerability to grow

*"The moment one gives close attention to anything,
even a blade of grass, it becomes a mysterious,
awesome, indescribably magnificent work in itself."*

HENRY MILLER

REG WAS a lawyer, and he was depressed. He came to our first session angry. He was angry he "had" to be there, working with a psychologist. "This whole thing is a waste of time. I should just be able to suck it up. What is the matter with me? Other people have had it much worse than me. I'm just whining."

When asked to describe how his depression showed up in his life, he said he was paralyzed with procrastination at work and felt numb much of the time. "I'm just going through the motions in my life." As he told me about feeling dead inside when his beautiful wife expressed love for him, Greg's face fell, and his shoulders slumped forward. I invited him to pay attention to his body. He said this was a pointless thing to do but grudgingly gave it a try. He described tension in his jaw and hands. When I asked him to tell me more about what he noticed he snapped, "I already told you." Greg became more irritated each time I encouraged him to look inside. Rather than slow down and feel what was going on inside, Greg relied on his idea of what was happening, based on a quick glance. He was impatient with himself, and when I gently pointed that out, he became impatient with me.

Your point of contact with vulnerability is a tender kernel framed by two forces: longing and limits. You yearn and you can't make it so. Your best efforts are thwarted, and you crash into "I can't." Emotion moves you. Whether you want it to or not, reality stirs anger or sadness or joy or guilt, and you don't get to decide which feeling or how intense or for how long it lingers. Have you ever wished you weren't so mad about something? Or didn't care so much about something? Or that you could ensure this blissful feeling would never end? Exactly.

But an amazing thing can happen in the place of "I can't." To feel helpless over something when you *are* helpless means to recognize the brick wall for what it is. You stop banging your head. You move through frustration to surrender. When you can take in the failure of your efforts, you can adapt. When you accept something is not possible, you can open to what *is* possible. You stop shaking your fist in the air and cursing the heavens. You stop ignoring yourself and shutting down your feelings and trying to be someone other than who you are.

There is utility in futility. When you register what doesn't work, you can correct course. Think of solving a maze: The trick is not in knowing the way through, because you cannot see that far ahead. The secret is being able to recognize a blind alley. The quicker you identify those, the quicker you can move on to the next path. Although there's much to be said for persisting, a point comes where continuing down a dead end is a waste of energy. When you see the blind alley of your limits, you can take a new path. You face reality. You accept yourself as vulnerable and are greeted by the miracle of your own growth.

As you surrender to reality, your intelligent body may signal with a beautiful gesture. I've witnessed it hundreds of times. Hands turn, ever so slightly, palms upward as people's bodies understand before their minds: "This is in the hands of something larger than my will." You reach a place to rest awhile, a still point after all the struggle. You accept what you *cannot* make happen and open to what you *can do.* You can pay attention to unrest, soothe the body, face your feelings, and live from the heart.

When we first meet, many people I work with unconsciously blame themselves for the hard things in their lives. Losses, frustrations, trauma, disappointing relationships—they see them all as evidence of some personal fault. Without realizing it, they reject themselves in their vulnerability. They act as though they had, or should have had, ultimate control over how things worked out. They are tied up in blame and criticism and anger with themselves. This is not the same thing as being accountable. They are trying to undo the unfortunate thing with fantasies of control, perfectionism, and over-responsibility. They avoid having to feel sad about what didn't work by feeling bad about themselves instead.

You'd think feeling bad about yourself would be worse than simply feeling sad about something not working out. But self-blame is a clever trick. It allows you to nurture the fantasy that you had the power to singlehandedly make it so.

You are magically made invulnerable. Thinking "I had control, I could have fixed it, and I just didn't try hard enough" gives you an illusion of power. But it's not reality. Because most of the time, you *are* doing the best you can with what you have at the time. Admitting that fact is vulnerable. What would it mean if you accepted that you tried your best? What if the outcome just wasn't entirely up to you? Are you still worth caring about? Do you still matter?

To recognize that we don't have complete control and need help stirs terrible feelings of being small and weak. These feelings are amplified when we reach out to another person. Old memories arise of how others in the past treated our hurts and needs. Those memories may not be conscious, but they show up in feelings of unrest, signaling anger and sadness and shame that lie underneath. The spike of unrest triggers a reflex to avoid, suppress, and shut down. So, we reject ourselves to get away from our discomfort.

Needing help, Greg rejected himself in vulnerability. Greg's *idea* of who he thought he should be was more real to him than who he really was. Every time we bumped into what he felt, a part of his mind judged him, making it unsafe for us to explore his vulnerable feelings. When I pressed him to stay with himself, he turned his impatience on me and the uselessness of therapy. His vulnerability was so shameful and unacceptable to him that he couldn't imagine anyone caring about him there. He couldn't let me accompany him nor pay inner attention, so he couldn't do the vulnerable work of therapy. He angrily rejected our work and himself.

Fearless

The importance of experiencing the point of contact with vulnerability has been percolating in my mind for decades. I was almost finished my PhD and had been working with patients suffering panic and anxiety for a few years when, in 1993, I was gobsmacked by the movie *Fearless*. Jeff Bridges plays Max, a man who believes he is invincible when he survives a catastrophic plane crash. He detaches from his vulnerability and begins to live as though he cannot die. Max is liberated from all sorts of challenging human predicaments, like when to tell a lie that might make someone feel better (never) and how to connect with others who have not lived through what he has (don't bother). He is free of all the inner discomfort of unrest. He is ecstatic with his freedom from fear.

Max experiences no conflict between what he wants and what he can have, because he believes he is invulnerable. If death can't stop him, nothing can. He walks without looking across a multi-lane highway, balances on the ledge of a skyscraper, and lives through eating a strawberry that should kill him with anaphylaxis. He thinks he is free, and he is euphoric.

But sadly, Max is not living a human life. He is untouchable, alienated. He is not resilient. Not having come to terms with what happened during the plane crash, he is in denial. His marriage suffers, and he hurts those close to him. His transformation back to humanity comes in a brilliant turn where (spoiler alert) he tries to help another survivor who lost her toddler in the crash, and nearly dies himself. His belief in his own immortality is shattered. When he goes home from the hospital, he eats a strawberry and has a massive allergic reaction. He is afraid and crying and joyful and shocked and reaches for his loving wife. He comes to life. He is vulnerable and beautifully human again.

In opening to longing, limits, and pain we become authentic, resilient, and intimate. Our humanity is tethered to our vulnerability. We unconsciously fear the pain of emotion signaled by unrest because it feels like we may die. But death is not in the pain; it is in the closed heart. The closing originally designed to save us is what extinguishes us.

Fostering Growth

Growth is not a matter of learning new ideas or gaining insight. It's not analyzing in novel ways or bringing a fresh perspective to your circumstances. Growth is deepening your capacities for living fully, which extend from allowing yourself to *actually feel* your experiences in your body. Your joy needs to lift and tickle you, your rage needs to burn, your guilt needs to twist in your core, your love needs to pull you forward, and your sadness needs to weigh upon your heart and rise up into your eyes as the pain melts into tears. When it comes to growth, emotion drives the bus. No matter how much your intellect yells from the back seat, the steering wheel is in your heart's hands.

Growth is a natural, organic process, so why do you need to take part in it? Since you are designed to grow, can't you just ignore yourself and let it happen? In fact, many of us do just that and get along fine. Growth happens. Often enough, with or without conscious participation, we do mature, at least to some extent. Things happen that move us, and our defenses do not block all that truth from our awareness. As we experience the flow of emotions evoked by life's ups and downs, we come to know who we are at a deeper level.

But perhaps you're not satisfied with the incidental, chance nature of just allowing life to do its thing and hoping growth happens to you. Maybe you want to be a conscious cocreator of your most authentic life. This book aims to awaken you to the amazing tool of unrest so that you can deliberately facilitate your growth. You have that power when you see the paradox of unrest. On the one hand, the discomfort of unrest unconsciously drives you away from what you feel, and on the other hand, its true purpose is to get your attention and invite you closer. Unrest heralds the engine for growth, and your willingness to feel emotion will actualize the most growth out of each life opportunity.

The bottom line is you must soothe unrest to get the maximum benefit of emotion. You can function and busy yourself and repeat all the affirmations you want, but if your body is feeling unrest and you leave it in that state, you won't feel safe enough to grow.

Change Is Not Growth

An acquaintance of mine many years ago was faced with a diagnosis of prostate cancer when he was in his late forties. He woke up. He gave up his decades-long smoking habit, switched his diet from processed to whole foods, and took up regular exercise. He began a mindfulness meditation practice to manage his chronic anxiety and high stress. He tended to be a hermit, but now decided to reconnect with friends and reach out for support. He apologized to people he had hurt with his sharp sarcasm and opened himself to greater intimacy. He spoke of having a deepened appreciation for small daily experiences of being alive, the smell of the earth after the rain, the song of sparrows outside his window, and the comfort of his bed. He had changed, and we all noticed it.

He received treatment, both chemotherapy and surgery, and fortunately recovered with a clean bill of health. Such a relief and joy for him and for all who cared about him. Within a year of his good news, however, he had returned to his old ways. He was turning down invitations and alienating folks with his biting humor when he did show up to socialize. He had begun to sneak cigarettes and junk food, and his old familiar pessimism reemerged. He had lost his ability to see the magic in everyday things. Nothing inside him had genuinely matured. Once the novelty of having faced mortality passed, he went back to the patterns he had practiced his whole life. The change did not stick.

Change is an alteration in something (a perspective, an attitude, a behavior), often triggered by some external situation. But alteration is not necessarily maturation. Change can be undone. In contrast, once you grow into a new stage, you cannot "ungrow." Growth cannot go backward. The sprout never goes back into the seed. Growth endures and brings you closer to who you are most deeply meant to be.

What Are You Growing, and Why Does It Matter?

We are meant to grow. All living things contain a unique blueprint seeking expression. Encoded, in part, in our DNA, this blueprint directs the expression of who we are meant to be. We each come with biological instructions for traits and characteristics that make us particularly ourselves. Even deeper in humans is a hunger, a calling from our soul for wholeness. We are meant to live grounded in our bodies, wholehearted and connected to others and the world. We are summoned to emerge from our self-conscious hiding, to come out from behind defenses and excuses, and live from the heart.

So what is it that *you* are growing? Here we will examine *authenticity*, *resilience*, and *connection*—three powerful capacities that expand when you face and feel your emotions. They underpin your mental health, enrich your quality of life, and open you to the vastness of your potential.

"The only way that
you'll actually wake up
and have some freedom
is if you have the capacity
and courage to stay
with the vulnerability
and the discomfort."

TARA BRACH

Authenticity

We often admire the ability of people to be genuinely themselves. When we sense that someone is real, without self-consciousness, we feel drawn to them, and their comfort in their own skin often helps us be more genuine, as well. Authentic people are okay with themselves in the complexity of who they are. Somehow these people have found a way to feel safe in being themselves. Not in a defensive, "to heck with what other people think" kind of way. But in a more "anchored in the body" way.

There is something so particularly human in the difficulty of truly being oneself. It is the gift and the curse of reflective consciousness. Without it, we would have no notion of being or not being ourselves. How ridiculous to wonder if a heron or a daffodil or your dog or any other creature in nature is being itself. These organisms simply manifest themselves as they are, without any need to hide or present a facade or deny the basic "isness" of who they are.

But we have a choice: We can deny ourselves. We can construct facades, hide behind words, and present only some facets of ourselves. We can do this consciously, but often we falsify ourselves outside our own awareness, when unrest triggers us. Rather than recognize the truth of our emotion and awaken, we sleepwalk into a wardrobe filled with costumes and masks and, in our somnambulant state, dress ourselves in ideas of who we are.

Emotion will guide you toward the answers to the big questions of your life. I know folks who post photos on Instagram and ask others to tell them which outfit to wear to the wedding or which movie is best for a first date, but really no one knows better than you, even when you don't 100 percent know. Your best guess is better than anyone else's big opinion. That is even truer with deeper and more important questions. You cannot have a straw poll or do an online survey to find out whether she is the right woman for you, or whether you should take that new position, or if or when you should request medical assistance in dying. These answers reside in your inner experience of emotion. Do you feel relieved or sad at the thought of losing her? When you imagine yourself leaving your current job, what do you feel? And what do you feel seeing yourself in the new position? What happens inside when you imagine being cognitively and physically impaired, dependent on others and unable to communicate? Do you feel some faith and hope about how you would find inner meaning despite limitations? Or do you feel that quality life would not be enough? You see, there is no right or wrong when it comes to what matters to you. It is what it is. And you are what you are, and you are (at a deep level) what you feel.

Being authentic is a form of personal power. When your self-esteem is not based on things you possess—your job title, the admiration of others, or even certain qualities—but on the congruence between your inner experience and its expression, you are truly potent. When you soothe unrest, you can access immediate information about yourself in the moment you are touched and moved by life. That living window onto your true self lets you know yourself and act on behalf of yourself from a place of integrity.

Resilience

Resilience is your capacity to come through the challenges of your life without hardening against your true self or the world. It is being able to bounce back after hardship, to get up one more time after falling down. It is persisting, but it is more than that. It's the ability to experience life fully in all its trials and come through still open and receptive. Resilient people are more protected from the viruses of self-doubt and shame via the immune system of their mind. Like immunity, resilience does not show up when things are going swimmingly. It shows up in the ways people treat themselves when things are *not* going right.

When you want to sustain your efforts, resilience helps you forge on when things are not immediately bending to your will. And it allows you to quit when you see that your efforts are futile. Resilience also allows you to try something new when it turns out that the route you've taken is off course. This is often at the heart of creativity, when you must find a new path after the original one is blocked.

Resilience is the holy grail of mental health, researched at universities all over the world. Resilient people are not incapacitated by the same events that cripple others. They have healthier bodies, more balanced emotions, more attuned communication, and are more flexible. They have greater insight and more empathy for themselves and others. The roots of resilience lie in having been cared for in childhood with warmth and interest. Held and soothed in their vulnerability as children, resilient people can now hold themselves.

To be resilient, you need to feel the vulnerability inherent in the experience of "I can't." You walk the empty void of what was not, what is not, and what cannot be. You must turn your attention inward, face and feel discomfort. Then you reorient, recognize what you still have, reclaim your energies and resources, and set out again on the next task or path. You get up one more time after being knocked down. And you matter all the while.

Resilience allows you to adapt to the challenges of being human with grace and courage and heart. So many of us live in the petrified forest of old, unfelt affliction, inured against others and ourselves. We use hard language for coping with adversity. We brace ourselves. We steel our will. We toughen up. We hunker down. And in our bodies, we are tempted to harden. We grit our teeth. We choke back our tears. We clench our stomach and clutch our fists. We tense and tighten and restrict the flow. We close off and shut down.

A healthy child, when hurt or frightened, can feel a rush of emotion without defenses and, when held in a caregiver's warm embrace, can express that emotion and move like quicksilver on to the next intriguing moment of the day. You too can be this resilient. The key lies in having confidence you can regulate unrest and stay with yourself as you feel what you feel.

Resilience is a kind of faith. Faith that even though you cannot make everything work out, everything will be okay in the end, because you can deal with it if you hold it in your soft strong heart. Resilience is not giving up on your soft heart, even as the world asks that it break now and again. It is trusting your broken heart will mend and knowing it's better breakable than not. An unbreakable heart is an untouchable heart. And such a heart cannot be moved. And what cannot be moved cannot grow.

Connection

The most beautiful and the most painful experiences in our lives revolve around close connections with other people. You are biologically wired to attach to others, and the ways you open yourself to closeness or shut yourself off from others greatly governs your quality of life. The health of your connections with others predicts depression, anxiety disorders, physical health, and even life expectancy.

Nothing activates vulnerable emotion like your longing for attachment. The opportunity for intimacy awakens hope, fear, joy and sadness, longing, love, and anger. As you feel the possibility of closeness with another, you are stirred by emotion and signaled with unrest. When you open yourself to connect intimately with others, you open yourself to being hurt. If you have no ultimate control over your emotional reaction, you most certainly do not control the emotional reactions of others. You may want their love and approval, but you cannot make that happen. And everything you do to shape how others see you keeps you at a distance from them. You are faced with a difficult choice. Soothe unrest, feel emotion, and risk sharing your real self with the chance of being rejected and alone; or hide yourself, engage superficially, and guarantee that you remain alone.

The word "intimacy" comes from the Latin for "innermost." Among your deepest desires is to be *seen and known* in the depths of who you truly are; among your deepest fears is to be *rejected* there. Many of us spend much of our lives oscillating between these two conflicting needs: trying to be seen and trying to hide. We build a facade to shield ourselves from the knowing glance, the eyes that see. We fear we will not be accepted or wanted in our real self. We say to ourselves, "If they really knew me..." or "If they saw the real me..." And we fill in the blank with some awful movie of being exposed and forsaken, found out as unworthy or unlovable. Yet it is precisely in that glance, being seen in the vulnerable truth of yourself, that your hope and healing reside. When you can soothe unrest and bear emotion, others can feel you with them. You are connected.

A Call You Need to Take

Growth is calling. Like a ringing telephone, it insists you answer. Unrest pings precisely as a vulnerable truth touches you, and your body asks for assurance it is safe. Only when your body knows you're not in danger can you drop down to the deeper levels of yourself and feel. And grow. You have a choice. You can answer the call and get the message, or you can dismiss it. You can let that call go to voicemail.

You know those alerts that you get from your phone to get your attention? That's what your bracing and fidgeting are trying to do: grab your attention. Just like your phone, unrest keeps at you, beeping and buzzing and dinging. More and more messages come through. But there is a limit to how many you can store. When the voicemail is full, the phone disconnects. When you ignore unrest, that's how you feel, too. Full, overflowing, jammed up, and eventually, disconnected.

I don't know what eventually happened to Greg. We worked together for several months, and despite small breakthroughs, the work was excruciating for both of us. Clearly, Greg knew that something did not feel right, which is why he reached out. I was hardly the first psychologist he had sought help from. And I believe he and I both were trying for all we were worth to help him out of the dark hole of his depression. Every time Greg tuned in to his sensations of unrest and his anxiety eased, or he opened to a small bit of emotion and his mood lifted, he rapidly dismissed those effects as trivial.

Like many people who survived early life by denying emotional pain in the body and escaping to the cooler reaches of the analytical mind, Greg steadfastly negated his inner experience. He met invitations to value his feelings of ease or uplift with disdain. I can only imagine how his tender feelings in childhood were met with much the same contempt, and he came to believe his survival hinged on maintaining that stance against himself. Sadly, although I hope seeds of mattering were planted for Greg to cultivate in the future, we were unable to break that abusive cycle together and he left therapy still rejecting himself.

What will it take for you to listen to unrest and answer its call? For some people the jammed-up feeling itself is pressing enough to convince them to tune in. For others, it takes some kind of backlash from the caller. Buried emotion threatens to break through. The body starts to act up with symptoms that become ever more difficult to disregard. Emotional and behavioral signals become increasingly difficult to ignore. Muscle twitches and aches, indigestion, sleeplessness, inflammation, headaches, panic attacks, and irritability clamor for attention. Eventually, people begin to realize that something doesn't feel right. They do not feel themselves.

Your Body Is Listening. Are You?

Your body is listening. And it is seeing and smelling and tasting and feeling this life of yours. It leaps to defend you and longs to wholly inhabit the living moment. It perceives changes in your blood flow and chemistry, it registers how you are oriented in space, it senses muscle tension and pain and hunger and balance, and more. And your body is tracking emotion. Vital to your development, your wise body tunes in to emotion as it rises and signals you with unrest so you can join in the conversation and grow.

Your body hears you also, in that busy mind of yours. Its ears prick up when you mutter threatening messages of not good enough, or don't have enough, or won't be okay. And it braces and holds its breath. You may already know that is a bad way to talk to yourself, and you may be trying to speak kindlier to yourself. But are you aware of the moment those thoughts arise, and what is happening in your body just before the unkindness is unleashed? Can you register the unrest that heralds your vulnerability that must be silenced with criticism and cruelty?

And even deeper, below your conscious awareness, your body senses your chronic exit from yourself. Ignoring your body is also a message to yourself. Looking outward and away, you distract and busy yourself and avoid the uncomfortable call. As you neglect your inner experience, your body mistakenly senses danger. It misperceives your external focus as evidence there is something threatening "out there" that needs to be tracked for survival's sake. So, your body stays on alert. With tensed muscles and held breath your body expends precious energy monitoring the world. It does this for you as an act of love, trying to keep you alive. But it longs for the day when the war is over, and you can come home.

PRACTICE: DEVELOP YOUR MUSCLES FOR TUNING IN

Of course, we cannot be attuned to our inner feelings every minute of the day. We have things to do, after all! But, since our bodies and brains are so inclined to look outward, actively tuning in to sensations is useful, to grow your ability to direct attention inward when you choose to. Set a reminder on your watch or phone to prompt you to focus on your physical sensations in that moment. When you are cued, turn your awareness toward muscle tension and notice where you feel tight and braced. Check your breathing and observe if it is relaxed or shallow. See if you can notice how your energy feels: is it smooth or jittery, calm or racing? Any sensation that you notice is a win for you. Give yourself credit for exercising your capacity to direct your attention where you want, when you want. That is success!

PRACTICE: CATCH UNCONSCIOUS UNREST

How often in a day do you find yourself mindlessly checking your phone? Is it possible right in the moment you grab the phone that you're provoked by unrest? Is there perhaps a flicker of something vulnerable and real rising? If you catch yourself grabbing for a distraction or occupying yourself mindlessly, what was there inside you in the split-second just before? Can you pause and step back that half-second and touch what was there? Some quiver or bracing or holding of your breath? Just tune in for a moment and register it. Wonderful! You are already changing your brain.

PRACTICE: WHAT IS YOUR RINGTONE?

Like your phone, unrest has a unique and personalized ringtone that lets you know it's just for you. All of us are signaled with constricted muscles and feelings of agitation, but your body sends you specific sensations that are particularly yours. Your job is to learn those signals so you can quickly respond to your call. Be curious, and really listen for your ringtone: the specific pattern of bodily sensations that arise when you are being invited to attend to your inner truth. You have hundreds of muscles, and some will signal more intensely with unrest than others. Note which muscles are most talkative when unrest signals you. Do you tap your toes or twiddle your fingers or clench your butt or bite your lip? Do you hunch your shoulders or hold your breath? Does your throat close or do your biceps tighten? Try to identify three sensations that are reliable indictors of unrest for you. That is your ringtone, and now you know what to listen for. Success!

Faith in the Power of Your Attention

Your body is calling to you with emotional truth, inviting you to grow. Life is meant to touch and move and affect you. You need to sustain yourself in the face of stress and be able to bend when you must. You need your heart open so you can face what you cannot fix and act on what you can. When you embrace unrest, you can bear emotion and grow your most powerful human capacities.

Tenderly hold yourself. Know you will feel unrest, and understand it is not danger. Stay with yourself in the quivering and tension and expect it will not be easy. Embrace the vulnerability at the heart of being human and have faith in the power of your attention to soothe your body. That is the work of growth. And you are so worth it.

5

retracing your path away from yourself

"History, despite its wrenching pain, cannot be unlived, but if faced with courage, need not be lived again."

MAYA ANGELOU

JULIE IS a joyful, dynamic, and quietly influential woman who completed therapy with me many years ago. She embraced our work of coming home to the body and successfully resolved her panic and anxiety problems, and now keeps in touch from the new city where she lives with her husband and two children. Julie is a wonderful mother who is now a leading force helping people listen to the body's wisdom through yoga practices. Working with me, she grew her capacity to soothe unrest and faced and healed deep unresolved feelings from childhood, and now she and her husband are the finest parenting tag team I have ever known.

Here is Julie's description of her daughter, her second child, at one and a half years old:

Everything is a whole-body experience for her right now. Someone pulls up at the house and she's so unbelievably excited to see them. Literally her whole body seizes up with delight. She stamps her feet, and she shakes. "Ooh, ooh," she exclaims, as her hands tremble and her face is lit with total joy. It's extremely gratifying to anyone who's pulling up at our house... Similarly, I might add, when I can't pick her up in that moment or I can't give her a toy she wants or a butter knife—which, by the way, she really enjoys knives right now—it's then a whole-body experience of another kind. She gets a total body experience of despair, where her hands go over her face and she wails and she collapses to the floor. And the thing is, she's just delicious in all her extremes.

Were you seen as delicious in all your extremes when you were little? The person you are today is the fruit of countless small moments in your early relationships. But the deep impact of your childhood experience is hard to see, and our society erects barriers to perceiving it. You look back with your adult eyes and find it difficult to imagine how seemingly small shortfalls of warmth or empathy or felt safety in childhood could have meaningful effects on you today. You navigated your needs with parents who did their best and now, for the most part, you are managing just fine. In this culture of "self-made" and "can-do," you are pressed to assume your childhood experience has little lasting impact on you today.

Yet encoded in your brain and relived today in unconscious reactions to your vulnerability and expectations about what you deserve are scores of small, forgotten exchanges with your caregivers. What happened when you were hungry, angry, scared, or longing to be held? What was the music of her voice? What was the look in his eyes and on his face?

In the dance of picking up and putting down were there gentle, easy movements? You have forgotten what it was like to be small and helpless and dependent on others. You adapted and survived, so now you look at the world and yourself through the lens of your adaptations. Yet buried beneath brain pathways designed to protect you from painful memories lies the knowledge of compromises made to your blossoming self.

The Big Deal About Being Small

The definition of dependency can be found in the breath-by-breath experience of being a baby. Unable to feed yourself, move independently, speak, or take care of your bodily functions, you would die in no time without attentive others. For this brief but crucial period of your life you are meant to be the center of the universe. And perhaps you were and perhaps you were not...

We learn who we are through the way we are treated. As adults we don't want to feel what this means because it is truly vulnerable. Not only were we small and helpless then, but we also are helpless now to undo what happened. Some people simply reject this connection between past and present to cut off the pain: "What's the big deal?" "What can I do about it now?" "What's the point of remembering or feeling that old stuff?" Others, overwhelmed as they realize the harm from childhood shortfalls, collapse into passivity and victimhood.

But you don't have to defend yourself or collapse when faced with this truth. Your challenges may originate in the past, but now you can pay attention to unrest, feel emotion, and rewire your brain. It takes courage to "connect the dots" of your life and mobilize growth today, but you are so worth it.

You Were Once a Baby

Even before birth, your brain was reaching out to experience the world and shaping itself to match it. Your brain was formed *in relation to* your environment inside and then outside the womb. At birth, your brain had close to one hundred billion nerve cells, or neurons, almost as many as there are stars in the Milky Way. Shortly after birth, in response to the sights, sounds, and sensations of the world, those nerve cells grew trillions more connections between one another, not all of which you needed. You had connections among parts of the brain that do not relate: between the part of the brain wired for hearing and the part of the brain wired for taste, for example. Retaining neural connections is a "use it or lose it" process. Since you don't have meaningful experiences linking what you hear with what you taste, those circuits atrophy while more useful pathways strengthen and grow. In neuroscience the expression for this developmental truth is "neurons that fire together wire together." Transmission along these circuits is made more efficient over time by a process called *myelination*, making it easier to do what you've done before, like traveling along a well-used road is easier than on an overgrown path.

Repeated experience sculpts the brain, priming you to continue to experience the world the way you did when you were small. This priming occurs at a level below your awareness, *in your body, not your conscious mind.*

As an infant and small child, you needed your parents' help to take care of your needs and feelings. When you needed something, physical or emotional, your muscles tightened, and you gestured for attention. Your heart rate and blood flow increased, and stress hormones flooded your system. You waved your arms gurgling and calling, then escalated to crying and shrieking and flailing if you got no response. Those physical expressions of arousal told your parents you needed help. Biological factors like temperament contributed to how easily you could internalize your parents' soothing, and your unique characteristics interacted with your parents' capacities in a small-step-at-a-time process, as you learned to care about and take care of yourself.

You absorbed your parents' emotional regulation as they shared your glee and dried your tears and calmed your anger and comforted your fears. Your later capacity to take care of your own emotions emerged out of these repeated experiences of mattering to them. Shoots of self-soothing capacity sprout up as early as toddlerhood. Your emotional capacity gradually developed, as you were held in the warm eyes and hearts and minds of your caregivers.

But what if a parent misses the cues and does not come? If a parent does not soothe you and instead punishes or shames or leaves you alone, your distress escalates. You are helpless and you are alone. Your developing brain links the feeling of life-and-death threat with a sense of utter abandonment. It is unbearable and it feels like you will die. You need to escape and there is no escape. Eventually, you stop protesting and shut down. You learn that you cannot bear what it feels like to be you. You learn to leave your body, to leave home when arousal rises.

This patterning of your emotional reactions is revealed in the automatic ways you relate to yourself and to others. You do not see the inner mechanisms designed to protect you from pain. Your response is involuntary. Your body knows, the way it knows how to ride a bike. You remember, but you don't really know *what it is* that you remember.

So it is with unrest. If, when you were distressed, your parent repeatedly came to you with soft eyes, gentle hands, and warm tones and patiently helped you to bring the distress back down, you come to expect that arousal simply works that way. You grow connections in your brain to reflect the confident expectation that what goes up will come down, and you live with an unconscious assurance that your feelings will not drown you. Although unrest still signals uncomfortably and prompts you to pay attention, you do not feel an urgent need to escape when it does. You treat unrest, and yourself, as important.

On the other hand, if your feelings were typically ignored or criticized or punished and you were left too long to marinate in a biochemical soup of stress hormones, today you will automatically escape your bodily arousal like it is a pack of hungry wolves.

The Hidden Lie: To Feel Vulnerable Is to Die

When a child is not soothed, feelings escalate and the brain kicks into emergency mode. The child is flooded and needs to escape the anguish. At a certain point, the child goes past fight/flight and is in a state of freeze. The brain shuts down in a dorsal-vagal response where the child appears calm but is numb. The freeze state mimics death and feels like death to a child's brain. Primitive and powerful, these mechanisms remove the felt sense of terror in the body. With repeated experience, this becomes a well-worn pathway in the brain. A devastating link is made: *to feel vulnerable is to die.* Repeated cycles of overwhelm forge connections deep in the brain, below conscious awareness, prompting you to avoid any signal reminding you of that devastating early experience.

Your conscious mind has long ago forgotten the experiences that set the stage for these unconscious biases, but your body remembers. Waking up and noticing your embodied automatic tendencies today allows you to retrace your steps away from yourself and begin to make your way home.

Attachment and Attunement

Attachment is a biological command to have closeness at all costs with those who take care of us. It is wired so deeply into us that in childhood it overrides all other needs. Children will jeopardize their own survival to try to get a parent back. They will stop eating and drinking and sleeping; they'll wail and scream; they'll run into traffic or into the dangerous night to chase after an abandoning parent. Preserving the attachment bond is as crucial to a child as life itself.

We need our parents close. This is physical, of course, but it is also emotional. We long to feel safe with them, we long to be seen by them, and we long to *feel felt* by them. But this instinct, wired into us for survival, sets us up to be hurt when our parents fail us in their attachment duty. We cannot ultimately *make* our parent come to us. Our reaching out and crying and protesting may influence them, but nothing we do can guarantee it. We need them and can't make them come and that is truly vulnerable.

Your parents' most important emotional job was keeping your felt sense of vulnerability within an optimal window. Like Goldilocks's porridge, your emotion needed to be held within a range of intensity that was not too hot and not too cold. You needed enough stimulation to feel engaged and safe, but not so much that you got overwhelmed. If your parents were emotionally skilled, they tracked your energy and modulated their own so you would not be overstimulated by their unregulated excitement, need, or distress, nor bored and shut down by their neglect.

Piglet sidled up to
Pooh from behind.
"Pooh?" he whispered.
"Yes, Piglet?"
"Nothing," said Piglet, taking
Pooh's paw.
"I just wanted to be
sure of you."

A.A. MILNE

Even as babies we can sense our parents' emotional tone. Meeting our basic needs is not enough. Our parent must *want* to come toward us and take care of us with warmth and interest so we can feel safe and secure. If they come to us but are impatient or angry or emotionally vacant, we feel alone and afraid. If they do not come at all, we may be terrified. The good news is (since none of us is perfect!) if a parent notices a child's upset and soothes it, there is a repair.

You can find a beautiful video on YouTube of the work in Ed Tronick's lab. In the video, he illustrates this magic of attachment, rupture and repair, using the "still face experiment" with a young mother. She engages with her one-year-old baby in a delightful back-and-forth game and is then instructed to stop responding to her baby's cues for her attention. She stills her face and disengages as her baby attempts to get her attention. The baby begins with little happy sounds that morph into louder calls and then shrill cries, and a look of confusion turns to terror as she goes from finger pointing to waving arms and then jerky spastic movements as though to fling herself in her baby carrier off the table.

The baby's distress is excruciating to watch, and although it is a matter of only a few minutes before the mother is instructed to engage again, it feels like forever for both the baby and the viewer. As soon as the mother shows up again as her loving, warm self, the baby begins to settle, and they reengage. As Tronick says, there is bad news in the rupture but there is good news in the repair, if the baby is not left too long in distress. In viewing the video, you can see that "too long" is not a matter of weeks or months but minutes, and although these exchanges may seem small from a distance, up close they are clearly shaping the child's brain.

Out of repeated brief ruptures and responsive repairs the child grows supportive connections in the brain that know ruptures aren't dangerous, they are temporary, and they can be repaired. "My efforts contribute to outcomes," the baby learns, "and I don't need to worry about feeling bad, because feeling bad does not go on forever."

Ethan, Julie's three-year-old son, fell and bumped his forehead. His eyes bugged out with the shock of the hurt and his breath was suddenly ragged. Julie could see he was winding up for a good cry and she was ready with a warm face and open arms to scoop him up. He looked into her tender face, sensed her well-regulated energy (not overwhelmed or too distressed), and suddenly brought his own hand up to his lips. Ethan kissed the palm of his hand and put it to the sore spot on his head and gently patted it while nodding his head and looking at his mother. Julie paused, close enough to gather him in her arms if he needed. Then after a moment he said, "I feel better now."

PRACTICE: YOU WERE A BABY ONCE

Imagine: you were a baby once. You will not remember in a conscious way all the small exchanges with your parents that shaped who you are today, but perhaps you can envision yourself as that small, helpless, dependent being filled with longing to be loved and safe. If you have a photograph of yourself as an infant, you could pull that out and gaze at your baby self. Open to the vulnerability of not being able to get even your most basic need met without the help of another.

As you reflect on this, notice what comes up for you in the here and now. Give yourself a moment to feel the sensations in your body. As you pay attention to your body and imagine being a wee baby, what feelings arise? Do you feel impatient? Irritated? Bored? Tender? Warm? Sad? Tired? Curious? Critical? Does your unrest shoot up high? Are you surprised at your reactions? Do you like how it feels to be with yourself? Or do you just want to stop the exercise and get away from your helpless baby self?

Be as open and curious as you can. There is no right or wrong with this practice. Anything you notice is success. Your reactions to paying attention to yourself today are rooted in how you were attended to long ago and provide clues to guide you in coming home to yourself in your vulnerable feelings today.

The Limbic System:
Mammals Are Different from Reptiles

What is the main difference between you and a snake? No, it is not your legs. Nor is it that you were not hatched from an egg into the world. It is your limbic system, the seat of emotions. As a result of the limbic system, the human brain is a social organ first. Your brain is structured with emotions to ensure you will take care of your immature young, not eat them. Where a reptile might walk on its own eggs to escape danger, a mammal will risk its own life to gather its young to protect them. This emotion-based bond creates the foundation for all meaningful experience in our lives.

The limbic system has a remarkable property: resonance. Like a tuning fork that picks up the vibration of a matching tuning fork ringing nearby, our limbic system can reverberate with other humans. We exchange emotional information through the music of our voices, the dance of our gestures, in our shared reflecting gaze. When you smile warmly at me, I feel your smile in my chest as it opens, in the curving corners of my mouth, and in my eyes as they crinkle and sparkle. I can feel your happiness in my own body, and I can feel your sadness and fear there, too. The physical experience of limbic resonance underlies the truth in the Swedish proverb "shared joy is a double joy; shared sorrow is half a sorrow." The miracle of attunement is how it lets us share and mirror and coregulate emotion for each other, fostering growth.

We need to feel attunement with our parents, to sense their emotional and biological rhythms. We become synchronized with our mother's breathing, sighing, blood pressure, appetite, sleep patterns, and energy levels. If we can join with her and she is well regulated, we feel good inside. If we cannot access her or if she is chaotic inside, our basic biorhythms are erratic, our internal sense of ourselves feels disjointed and out of control. The lack of emotional attunement leads to brain changes designed to protect us from what that feels like. But in later life, those adaptations unconsciously inhibit us from fully experiencing our feelings.

Effective parents read their child's inner state by attuning to their own body and picking up shifts in their own physiology. In other words, parents' own interoceptive capacities allow them to be there for the child in the way the child needs. Your parents' capacity to notice and respond to inner shifts in your breathing, muscle tension, blood flow, vocalization, and movement formed a foundation for you to eventually notice these signals in yourself, unaided. If, as you were picked up to be fed, your parent was warm and happy to be caring for you, your brain took in, "I'm not too much, my needs are not bad, taking care of my needs and emotions is good, and the world thinks so, too." But if your parent was irritated and exhausted and did not coo or smile or gently cradle you, you learned, "I am a burden, my needs are bad and evoke rejection, I don't deserve care, and the world doesn't care about me."

These micro-exchanges happened dozens and hundreds and thousands of times as your brain was maturing, each teaching you that you matter, or you do not. Neurons were firing together and wiring together, and today, from deep inside brain pathways created out of those exchanges, unconscious signals tell you being vulnerable is okay and leaning toward unrest to feel emotion is okay. Or it is not.

Having Experiences and Holding Ourselves

The limbic system is the seat of emotion, and the cortex is the home of intellect. The cortex is where we access thinking, will, reasoning, analyzing, planning, and awareness. And we love all these shiny gadgets. But many of us tend to overvalue intellect. We believe our minds should control our hearts and live as though ideas matter more than feelings. Don't get me wrong. I love my thinking brain. I love the swooping arc of thoughts as they fly me to new realms and carry me to imaginary times and places. I enjoy dissecting an argument and nailing down an idea with words. But if I am not grounded in the truth of my feelings, I can be tripped up by my high-flying ideas and fall flat on my face. Think of my spectacular face-plant of a first marriage. My idea that it was sound could not have held up for all those years if I had made room for the truth of what I felt. My feelings burbled and called to me from underground streams, and because I ignored them, I was stuck and suffered. But at the end, when my emotions were laid bare, my actions were life affirming and liberating.

If you imagine that your logic and willpower run the show, you are wrong. Your cortical brain obeys signals from below, from the physiological control centers of the reptilian brain and the emotional limbic brain. Over the span of our species' history, the emotional brain has been cueing us to what matters since long before we grew this rational brain, and in times of crisis it pulls rank like an older sister and over-rides your logical mind. We need all our resources to live fully, and it's time to get out of the faux either/or battle between logic and emotion and embrace our complexity in a way that empowers us.

Fortunately, in the thin outer layer at the front of the cortex sits the *prefrontal cortex*. This extraordinarily powerful part of your brain can observe and reflect upon your inner experience, both your thoughts and your feelings. The prefrontal cortex allows you to bend your awareness back upon itself. It lets you think about thoughts, think about feelings, feel about thoughts, and feel about feelings. You can think a thought and reflect, "I need to think that through more fully" or "I wonder why I feel so annoyed with her?" or "I am happy that I thought about that" or "I am sad about being so sad right now." It is where you hold the multilayered complexity of your experience.

The prefrontal cortex also lets you hold two opposing thoughts or feelings simultaneously. You can know, for instance, that you love someone and at the same time are so mad you want to throttle him. Both feelings exist and neither erases the other. In the "both/and" you are momentarily paralyzed, unable to act, and in that moment something new emerges that contains both realities. In your love for him, you cannot throttle him, and in your anger, you cannot ignore what's wrong. In your complexity, you can address the rupture with compassion and assertion, and repair it.

Your prefrontal cortex allows you simultaneously to feel unrest and know you are not in danger. Holding this complex thought is key to embracing unrest. If you only think analytically, either you are right to feel unrest because there is danger, or you are wrong to feel unrest because there is no danger. One fact displaces the other. If you feel afraid, then there must be danger, so figure out what it is and run away; or if you are not in danger, your feelings are silly or wrong, so shame on you and stop feeling that way. This dichotomy offers no room for the multifaceted richness of your vulnerable experience.

When you pause and reflect on your experience of unrest you access an integrated place where both things are true, and both matter: "I feel afraid and there is no danger." Yes, you are aroused with unrest, the surge of energy that *feels like* danger… and yet there is no danger. There is nothing wrong and nothing wrong with your feelings. Unrest invites you home right in this moment. Compassion blossoms and you grow.

PRACTICE: HOLDING BOTH LONGING AND NOT HAVING

Pick up your smartphone and be ready to record yourself. Now take a moment to ask, "What do I want right now that I do not yet have?" Choose something important to you that you cannot singlehandedly obtain, something that depends on help from someone else or whose timing is not in your control or has some other factor that limits your attaining it.

Really focus on how much you want what you want. See vividly both what you long for and the fact that obtaining it is not entirely in your hands. Wait until your inner vision is clear enough that your body begins to physically feel the longing, and the not having. Center yourself in your video frame and start your video. Say out loud:

"I want _____ and I do not have _____."

Say this aloud several times as you look into the camera. Then say aloud:

> **"Something that matters to me is not
> 100 percent in my control."**

Tune in to the physical sensations that arise. Pay attention to any tension or tightness, noticing where in your body the muscles are activated.

Turn off the camera and play the video back. Pay attention to what happens inside you as you bear witness to your longing and limits. Can you feel both feelings? Do you feel unrest?

Notice if your mind tells a story to magically deny your limits by pretending that you have control: "If I can't make it happen then I'm a loser." Or "I will make it happen no matter what." Notice too if your mind tries to deny your longing by painting it as trivial or hopeless. "There is no point in wanting that. I can never have it."

See if you can hold both your longing and your not-yet-having as equally true and equally important. Can you breathe into that space and feel the complexity inside you? What happens when you do that? Do you notice any shift in your physical tension? Ask yourself, "What is it like for me to hold both these things in my heart and mind right now?" Anything you notice is success, because you are training your brain to stay complex and hold the richness of your inner truth.

It Takes Two

As a child, you *needed* someone to see your inner experience and send an accurate image back to you to help you deal with feelings. The important people in your life "loaned" you the use of their frontal lobes to bring down emotions that were too big for you to handle. That older, wiser other would "digest" your experience and feed it back to you like a mother bird feeds her babies. Being mirrored back in your feelings helps you to see your inner experience, internalize care, and eventually give care to yourself as Ethan did when he kissed his hand and put it to his forehead. As you reached puberty and grew into early adulthood your own prefrontal cortex came online as neural pathways linked your emotion centers to the higher cortical function of reflection. That rewiring lets us reflect on and care about our own inner experience so we can handle emotions without needing another person, although it is always wonderful to have a compassionate other to accompany us.

If you lacked mature parents, you may not have known how to process your big feelings. Feelings of anger or sadness or closeness can make us feel dependent and shameful. The people who come into my office often find it excruciating to admit they have trouble regulating the feelings that flow inside them. They feel they "ought" to be able to do this, and experience shame and anxiety about being shut down or seeming out of control. They often keep a heavy lid on what is going on inside. They are using the defensive strategies they developed earlier in life to keep feelings away. But when we understand the power of interoception, when we tune in to unrest with warm interest and nonjudgment, we become that older wiser other for ourselves, and grow our ability to feel and deal.

Shannon's husband had died a few years earlier, and her two adult daughters were grown and out of the house. Alone and "lost," she was struggling with sleepless nights and long days without purpose. "I'm a worrier," she told me, "always on guard, my body always tight, migraines and sore neck and back aching all the time."

As I invited her to open up and notice herself in the moment with me, she said, "I don't want to focus on me or to need help. I keep things to myself. Nobody wants to hear my problems." Despite her habit of neglecting herself, Shannon agreed to pay attention to her unrest. She noticed pressure in her chest and spasms in her low back. Her stomach was flipping and her arms and shoulders were tense. She said she'd felt tense her whole life. But just as we started connecting with her inner discomfort, she said it felt like just one more example of her weakness—further evidence of being a failure.

I coached her to notice that critical message as a judgment, an opinion rather than a fact, and asked if she might let us experiment to see what would happen if we stayed with her discomfort. We continued to focus on sensations and after about five minutes Shannon lifted her eyes and they were shining. "I don't feel so tense," she said with surprise. "I gave up a long time ago, I never expected anything good could come of feeling. I disowned my body at around three years old and I've just been biding my time ever since." Shannon shared that her father had been a violent raging force throughout her life, had beaten her mother while pregnant with her and had slapped, yanked, shaken, and yelled at Shannon with hate in his eyes over and over when she was a small child.

The next week Shannon came in feeling a little bit hopeful, saying, "I gave up on myself, but it looks like I'm still in there." She spoke about living her whole life feeling she wasn't wanted and should never have been born. She remembered her mother's exhausted face and impatient voice and feeling rejected by her. We tracked her unrest and as it waned, she felt anger rise. Her unrest shot up immediately and she became anxious. "I don't want to feel angry," she said. "That would make me just like my father, ugly and out of control." We blocked that story and redirected her attention to the unrest.

After a few tries, her unrest dropped, and her anger emerged as a physical experience in her body. She stayed with it. Shannon's breathing became deeper, she sat up straighter and spoke with a stronger voice. "I have lived my life scared to feel," she said. "I got stuck in survival mode behind a wall I built to be safe when there *was* no safety. *They* were supposed to keep me safe."

The next week Shannon told me she said no to a last-minute request from her daughter to babysit, and set a limit with her housekeeper—two people she typically tried to please. As we investigated further Shannon felt strong and solid in her body, then suddenly her unrest shot up high. She had a weird sense of her feet and ankles lifting off the floor as though her body were trying to levitate. Shannon's unrest had tipped over the threshold where we could stay with sensations, and she was in red-light territory, where she needed to put a hold on arousal. (We will talk more about the traffic-light system in the next chapter.) Her mind was racing, and she was feeling floaty and dissociated.

I asked Shannon to observe that she had just felt assertive and powerful and solid, and then she got kicked out of herself. It was as though the emotion police had arrived and tasered her with a jolt of anxious high arousal. As soon as she could stand back and observe that her feelings had activated high unrest, Shannon settled. We returned to tracking unrest in her body and reinforced her skill at noticing and soothing what she felt.

We worked slowly, carefully over many sessions to peel back the layers of self-rejection and neglect until Shannon began to connect with herself in an immediate, physical way. Little by little she went from lost to found. She came to see that her original self was full of love and joy, that she came into this life ready to love and be loved, but the chaos and pain of those early years had severed her connection with that.

"It's time to realize that who I thought I am, isn't who I am. I am not that rejected, unwanted child. I thought I existed just to be small and make things okay for those parents. I was sucked dry by them. I need to take back my life and my light, and not keep shutting down and giving my life force back to them."

A sudden wave of nausea hit Shannon as she said this, a sign her unrest had shot up too high again, and we immediately tuned in and paid attention to bring it down. I asked Shannon to imagine her tense muscles as small, frightened beings trying to get her attention. She initially felt impatient and frustrated with herself, and I invited her to notice if there might be a critical voice inside her ramping up the arousal. She initially said she didn't think so, but when, after several minutes, her attention did not reduce her muscle tension, I asked again.

Shannon replied, "I guess I'm saying that I shouldn't have said anything bad about them. That I am the bad one, not them." Could she stand back from that self-attack, I wondered, and see it as something she might have thought as a small, helpless child. She nodded her head vigorously, so I asked her to look at things right now through her adult eyes, and then evaluate if that critical belief still seemed true. "Gosh, no!" she exclaimed.

"So now, let's be here in this moment as fully grown adults together and tune in again. We are looking at what you feel with warm interest, and we are not judging you at all, okay? Say hello to any place that is holding or tight or bracing or agitated. Tell me what you can feel in your body, where do you feel pressure or tightness?"

As she described what she felt—"My neck is so tight it's burning and my whole body wants to curl up in a ball"—I encouraged Sharon to stay with it, despite the discomfort.

"Breathe into it and invite each one of those places in your body to tell you all about what it is like for them right now." One by one she described the sensations with words like "tight" and "trembly" and "knotted," and then she articulated what that next experience felt like ("like there are ropes strapped across my chest"). Each level of description went deeper into her experience, from "jammed up and constricted" to "sore and achy" to "beginning to let go" as the tension began to ease.

After a few more moments she described a big release of energy and a feeling of strength and hope: "I've been on a long journey, but I feel like I'm going to like who I find at the end." She had a sense of a whole lot of little selves emerging and coming together inside her. "I feel bigger, like there's more me, and like I know where I am."

Not Blaming Mother (or Father) or You

Children are resilient beings. They are vulnerable but not fragile. They do not need parents who are perfect. In fact, an *occasional* gap in attention allows a child to step in and fill it with their growing capacities. Children need consistency rather than constancy. When a parent is available in a warm and interested way *more often than not*, the child comes to expect that they are worth paying attention to and caring about.

Parenting is the hardest and least appreciated job on the planet. Parents typically try their best to give their children better care than they themselves received. Each generation seems to want to offer their offspring a better chance at life. It is a daunting and hopeful task. Our parents parented us from their own inner capacities for attunement and regulation. They were probably working around injuries, sometimes giving from depletion, and often loving us as best they could. They will have failed, some more than others, in fully facilitating our sense of safety and mattering. This is not to blame them. It is simply to say that the work left undone inside you today *needs to matter to you.*

I want to shift a common theme I hear from my patients: blame, of self and other. "What's the matter with me?" "I should be over this." "My struggle with how my parents treated me is my fault." This doesn't help because the self-attack leads to self-neglect, passivity, and hopelessness. The other refrain I hear is, "They did their best, so I can't blame them. I need to suck it up and forget about it." This doesn't help either because, although it is probably true your parents did their best, you still have work to do to rewire your brain and emerge whole now.

Perhaps we can stop blaming and look instead at responsibility. This work is not about blame or forgiveness; it is about facing reality in all its complexity and tolerating the mixture of feelings that arises. When you were a child, your parents were responsible for providing the best environment to grow you to your full potential. You can hold them to account in your heart and mind for their strengths and successes as well as for their shortcomings. But today, as an adult, you are responsible for doing the same for yourself. Nothing else really matters.

All this focus on history is not meant for you to look backward, but rather to help you see how you acquired the habit of tuning out your signal for growth. The issue now is not what happened long ago but what you can do today to soothe unrest so you can grow.

PRACTICE: TRACK YOUR EXITS

Over the next week, pay attention to the times when you find yourself caught up in activities and behaviors that you haven't consciously chosen to engage in. This is not easy because exits can be so automatic. Be patient with yourself. But see if you can tell when what you are doing is motivated less from a desire for it and more as an escape from unrest...

See if you can turn the clock back to the split-second just before you clicked that link or grabbed the bag of chips or played that game of solitaire or poured that big glass of red wine. This is a remarkably slippery and quick moment, so no problem if it is hard to find. To even tune in and be curious is success. Most of us are sleepwalking away from home. But keep practicing until you can catch the moment when your shoulders hunch or your thumbs fidget or your chest freezes tight. And if you notice that, say hello to those feelings with warm interest and give yourself a pat on the back. You are on your way home.

6

coming home
to your body

"The body is a sacred garment..."
MARTHA GRAHAM

"I DON'T EVEN know why I've called you," Anita told me over the phone. "I don't know if I can trust anyone." Self-doubt and procrastination motivated her to seek out therapy but, having reached out, they were now worse than ever. Anita was on shaky ground.

Her first session started with her eyes darting everywhere but at me. A tiny smile froze her lips as she fiddled with her curly red hair that made her look much younger than her thirty-eight years. "Can you tell me more about what you'd like my help with?" I asked. As she crossed her legs, her upper foot flexed and locked in place. She held her breath, silent, and continued averting her gaze. After a few minutes, I gently asked her again and she shook her head. It had taken all Anita's courage to show up for the appointment with me. It was clear that until we addressed the unrest in her body, we would not be able to access Anita's issues. "Are you aware that your body is anxious right now?" Anita shook her head no. I explained how unrest activates our bodies to invite us to come home, and Anita was intrigued.

We turned our attention to the muscles locking her in place and identified where she was bracing. "Wow, my whole body is tense!" she exclaimed. We shared a moment of joy at her success in recognizing she was in a body, and then I invited her to look at one area at a time with precision. "I feel a bit tight in my neck," she said, "and maybe my shoulders are a little tense." As we worked together Anita repeatedly qualified her observations with "a bit" and "maybe" and "I'm not sure, but..." So I asked her, "What if you let those minimizing words go and just say what you feel in your body?" She stumbled and paused and second-guessed as though she were not allowed to matter enough simply to declare her own experience. It was like she was not the authority on herself. Her eyes pleaded, as if asking me to give her permission or to tell her what she felt. I waited and nodded and gently mirrored her as the expert on her inner world.

Each time she shared what she felt inside, we stayed with the feeling for a few moments longer, and Anita was surprised to find even more detail. The tension initially felt like pressure, and then the pressure felt like a weight on her. As we stayed with it the tension lessened and became a focused point over her heart, and she began to feel sad. As we cycled through these steps a few times Anita's face softened and, shyly, she said, "I think I can do this." We shared a delighted laugh, but then she blushed and looked away, as though she had revealed too much. She clammed up, anxiously scanning the room, avoiding my eyes. She was overwhelmed.

"What's it like to be with me right now?" I asked. It took several tries but eventually she admitted that she thought I was judging her, and it made her feel unsafe. "What's the evidence of me judging you?" Anita said she had felt close with her previous therapist but was betrayed. She was superimposing a mental movie of her previous therapist onto our session. I asked her to see if she could put that movie aside for now and notice what it was like to be with *me*. I invited her to feel inside her body, so she could learn more about herself and me.

"I don't want to let go of my suspiciousness," she replied. "It's like a map. It will keep me safe." I asked her, "Do you feel safe right now?" We both laughed because obviously she was in her old movie, bracing with high anxiety and not feeling safe at all. I told her about an old military expression. "When there's a discrepancy between the map and the terrain, trust the terrain," I said. "The 'map' is the story you're telling yourself. The 'terrain' is what you feel in your body in this moment with me. Would you like to focus on what is *really* happening right now?" Anita nodded, and as she tuned in and carefully felt the unrest, her body settled. Right then and there, Anita knew she felt okay in her body with me.

The Evidence You Are Safe Is in Your Skin

When do you most need to feel grounded in your body? When you are vulnerable. Yet when do you least *want* to give yourself the attention that would ground you? When you are vulnerable. When your longing meets your limits, emotion rises. Unrest heralds your point of contact with vulnerability and invites you home to the solid ground of your body, yet it feels vaguely threatening. If you ignore unrest, your body doesn't know it is safe and you escape the discomfort with defensive thoughts and behaviors. If you avoid what you feel, your body can't discover the things that move you are only feelings, not saber-toothed tigers.

After several rounds of noticing and soothing unrest, Anita, having long struggled with self-doubt and procrastination, left that first session feeling more effective than she had in years. Our work showed Anita she was both capable of and responsible for taking care of her unrest. Anita saw how she'd been acting as if she didn't know herself, looking outside for the answers. When she understood unrest as her call to come home, Anita stepped up to comfort her body with attention. She was pleased with her ability to hear her body's bid for attention and practiced feeling her unrest between sessions. When unrest signaled vulnerability with a tight neck or held breath or hunched shoulder, Anita turned toward her inner experience with warm attention.

Self-doubt had been a paralyzing prison for Anita but coming home to her body gave her the confidence she needed to get free. Session after session we activated feelings of vulnerability as we examined issues from work and her relationships and especially her reactions to being the focus of our attention. Instead of averting her gaze and second-guessing herself and going mute, Anita began to slow down when unrest signaled her and took care of it with patient, precise attention. Through repeated practice, she came to experience herself as the expert on Anita, starting with what it feels like inside. Acknowledging her competence made Anita feel powerful. She grew her ability to tolerate painful feelings and faced her anger and grief at losing the care and support of her prior therapist. The strength she gained from facing those feelings allowed her to address earlier betrayals of trust that had brought her to seek help in the first place. As she trusted herself more, she became less mistrustful of others, knowing she could stand up and speak for herself. She was no longer paralyzed with procrastination and self-doubt. She sought a promotion at work and progressed in her relationship with her partner. Anita was on solid ground.

Using Little Moments for Big Transformations

Unrest cues you to your points of contact with vulnerability. These don't have to be big or life-altering events. Little moments of vulnerability pop up daily, a wealth of growth opportunities if you know how to look.

Unrest calls you with a tight chest and racing heart as you realize, "I am late." How could paying attention to such a mundane experience be useful? It's counterintuitive to tune inward when it seems you should be hurrying to your destination, but you commit to being with your body as it asks for attention. You don't try to fix anything; instead, you say hello to the constriction and feel how fast your heart is beating. You spend perhaps a minute until the pressure in your chest eases and your heart rate settles. You breathe deeper. You are more in the moment. That's a win. You're already more yourself! Yet now you notice your shoulders have dropped and your triceps are tense. You recognize your anger emerging from underneath the unrest. You've been taking on more than your share, and others have been happy to let you. Your triceps want to push back against unreasonable demands on your time. The drop in your shoulders opens your chest and you feel bigger and more entitled to take your space. You decide to move efficiently to your meeting, but not add one more bit of stress or strain to yourself on the journey. You are not racing to please others, you matter.

Or perhaps, as you walk in the park near your home a small reddish dog intoxicated with joy rolls deliciously in the grass, and you notice yourself bracing and holding your breath. You check in and slow down and feel the tension constricting your neck and chest. You have the urge to turn away, but you stay with the tension in your chest until it lets go and you can breathe easier. As the unrest subsides, a memory of playing just like that with your own beloved companion bubbles into your mind. The sadness rises as you feel the pain and loss you've tried to ignore by not letting yourself think about her. Your throat tightens and your chest aches and there is pressure around your eyes. It hurts. But you lean toward the pain and feel it, and grief carries you from your guarded place of closed-off numbness to somewhere alive. You find yourself remembering her. Remembering your love for her and feeling tender delight and gratitude for the gift of the time you had with her. You feel larger inside because you have made room for love. And you have made room for more you.

Or you're waiting for medical test results and notice your clenched stomach and fidgety hands. Your concentration is shot, your nerves are on edge, and you're pacing up and down. You want to get away from yourself, go to the Internet to research diseases. Or eat chips or chug a beer. Maybe you get lost in a binge of Netflix. You recognize these as your old habits to avoid unrest and choose to come home. You block your exits and bring awareness to your agitation and muscle tension. You go slow and then even slower until your body settles. Then, in that bit of relief, you sense anger rising at the awful unfairness of uncertainty. Your back is straight, your jaw is set, and your fists are clenched. Your wave of anger is hot as it peaks, and your mind looks for someone to fight or blame or challenge. But there is only reality itself, and it doesn't care that you think this is unfair. Frustration bubbles and simmers and you stay with it until it ebbs. Rather than blame the system or yourself, you surrender and face your limits. Sadness rises. This is so painful. You want to be healthy, and you don't want to wait any longer for an answer. Yet there is nothing to be done. The sadness rolls over you and lifts you and drops you, again and again. For a few moments after your tears there is only stillness and quietness. Compassion fills you. The kindness that flows comforts you and bolsters you for the answer when it comes. You don't have ultimate control, but you are with yourself and that is powerful.

The path to growth can be traveled in so many ways, every day, when you know what to look for and what to do.

Say, "I DO": Identify, Describe, and Observe

I have invited you into a love story, with yourself. I have asked you to engage in a conscious relationship with the brilliant intelligence of your body as it signals transformational moments. You see now how you "have" your experience of unrest and vulnerability in your body and "hold" it in the reflective awareness of your prefrontal cortex. To have and to hold. So now, my dear reader who is both consciousness and matter, commit to joining inner forces and say, "I DO." *Identify*, *describe*, and *observe* your physical sensations in the moment of your vulnerability and enter the most important relationship of your life.

Identify (Green Light, Yellow Light, Red Light)

When unrest stirs, you can learn to track patterns of tension and activation. This guidance arises out of the work done by many gifted clinicians in the field of experiential dynamic psychotherapy, beginning with Habib Davanloo. Remember the map and terrain metaphor we discussed earlier? Think of this instruction as the general map and your own experience as the precise terrain. The terrain of your experience is your most important guide.

You have green-light, yellow-light, and red-light locations orienting you to unrest. In this step you are mainly just identifying *where* the sensations are located.

Green light means your unrest is in your somatic nervous system, which connects your brain to your voluntary muscles. Remember, those are muscles you can activate at will.

They enable you to move and give you structural and postural support. When you pay close, warm attention to voluntary muscles, they will often release themselves, at least slightly, after a few moments. *Yellow light* means your unrest is elevated and in your smooth muscles, which control changes in your blood vessels and organs and digestive tract. Because these muscles are primarily under control of the autonomic nervous system, they are slower to respond to your attention. *Red light* means your unrest is making your thoughts race out of control and making you feel dissociated from your body. This arousal is too high, and you need to deactivate mechanisms that are raising your body's sense of threat to a level that is too high for attention alone to soothe.

But you are not a cookie, and this approach is not a cookie cutter! Your *way of being toward yourself* is the key: Pay warm attention and stay open and curious. Do not criticize or judge any reaction you notice. You are the only you. No single set of instructions applies for all people or even for one person all the time. How your body responds to your attention is the guidance you need to stay the course or revise your intervention. If your body lets go, you are doing what you need to soothe unrest, and if it does not, step back and really listen for what your body is trying to let you know. At the end of this chapter, I will give you guidelines for tracking when you are on or off course and offer ways for you to come home if you have wandered away.

Perhaps the most challenging thing about this engagement with yourself is how very slowly you need to go to connect. Can you spend ten seconds being fully tuned into your tight neck? Can you stay with that discomfort without wriggling into a story about it? That is harder than it sounds, and it is key to everything that follows.

Green Light

Unrest tries to signal you first through your somatic nervous system's activation of your voluntary muscles, making them feel tight, constricted, and agitated. You might find yourself fidgeting with your hands or bouncing your leg. You might hunch your shoulders or clench your butt. Your biceps may tighten, or your back might be braced.

You have more than six hundred such muscles in your body, from your head to your toes and everywhere in between, and these muscles make up between 40 and 50 percent of your total body weight. That's a lot of real estate and although you may be tense "everywhere," you cannot soothe unrest in a general way. You need to pay precise attention to one area at a time.

Try to think of your body in groupings—shoulder, back, buttocks, legs, arms, hands, chest—and then break those groups down further into smaller muscles, if you can. So, for example, when you notice your legs are tense you might then differentiate the quadriceps and shins in the front of your legs from the hamstrings and calves in the back of your legs. If you notice your feet, be aware if the toes are pressing down into the floor or pulling up and away from the floor. The more precise you can be in focusing on just one area at a time, the clearer it will be to your nervous system that you are truly paying attention.

Yellow Light

If you miss unrest when it activates your voluntary muscles or if your emotional trigger is larger, your autonomic nervous system activates your smooth muscles. Those are the involuntary muscles connected with digestive, cardiovascular, and respiratory functioning. The mobilizing force of your sympathetic nervous system sparks you with adrenaline, jolting your heart to beat faster and pound harder. Your breathing speeds up to deliver oxygen to your large muscles. The saliva dries up in your mouth and throat, and it may feel hard to speak or swallow. Your eyes get dry. You may blush or tremble or shiver as goosebumps rise on your skin. Your armpits or palms or soles of your feet may sweat. You may feel nausea, bladder or bowel pressure, stomach gurgling, gas, and other gastrointestinal sensations.

This activation may be subtle, with just a tinge of these sensations, or more intense. It is a great success when you notice yellow-light sensations and can be life changing when you understand their message for you. You are not sick or bad or crazy! These sensations are just letting you know you missed the first level of signaling and your brain is running ahead of you. Sometimes that omission happens because you are just so tough and hard on yourself that pain is the earliest signal on your "to be noticed" list.

It takes a lot of practice for stoic people to correctly identify unrest in the body, and that becomes even harder if you believe it is weak or harmful to pay inner attention to what you feel. Sometimes your body goes into this high arousal because you are making up scary stories of illness or social threat or other danger. We will address this reaction in more detail when we look at defenses in chapter eight.

Red Light

If you miss the yellow-light activation of your smooth muscles, the dampening force of the parasympathetic nervous system can kick in to bring you back down with cognitive signals of overwhelm. When that happens, you could feel lightheaded or dizzy. You might have a dropping sensation like you are going to faint. Your legs might feel weak and jelly-like and your body may lose its muscle tone and seem to sag.

This is going into a red-light zone and, if you can, you must hit the brakes.

When unrest goes red-light, your brain stops working properly. Like Shannon in the previous chapter, you disconnect from your body and have trouble concentrating or thinking clearly. Your vision may be blurry, and you might hear ringing in your ears. You probably will have trouble following what someone is saying. Your thoughts are jumbled or racing. You may feel as though you're floating away or looking at the world through Plexiglas. For some people this cognitive distortion only happens during a panic attack or under severe stress. Some people, though, often those who have lived through childhood trauma, spend a lot of time in this removed state. And unfortunately, focusing on unrest is hard when your thoughts are disjointed and racing. The tool you use to track and soothe your body, your reflective capacity, is disrupted.

Once you're in red-light mode, you must pause, take a breath, and take the pressure off. Your job is to recognize you are cognitively "offline." Instead of locating unrest on the inside, you need to locate yourself in the outside world. That means looking around you and describing three things you can see, three things you can hear, and three things you can touch. State where *you* are located, such as "in my living room at home" or "in the vegetable aisle at the grocery store." You need to be assured that there is no threat in the here and now. When you know you're not in danger you can return to feeling sensations in your body. You can get back to a functioning brain, but you need to be patient as you cycle through the steps: tune in to sensations of unrest, notice you are detached, orient to the external world, and recognize the safety of the present. Then tune in to your sensations again.

You won't typically have all these green-, yellow-, and red-light reactions, and your experience will vary from one instance to the next. But your body likely has its favorite ways of trying to get your attention, so it is useful to familiarize yourself with your unique signal.

Please keep in mind that none of these green-, yellow-, or red-light sensations are "symptoms." They do not indicate anything pathological or bad or wrong with you. Even if your muscles hurt, they are not doing anything "wrong." Even if your digestion goes off, it does not indicate illness. Even if your brain temporarily gets spacey, it does not mean you have lost your mind. They are just escalating ways unrest is trying to get your attention. People often come to me with fears about illness arising from unrest. Unrest is not illness. Of course, if you continually ignore yourself and never soothe unrest, these reactions can be harbingers of future health issues. So, it is important for you to take this first step and tune in to locate unrest in your loving body.

Describe (Giving Language to Tension and Energy)

Once you've located *where* the unrest is in your body, you describe *what* the sensations feel like. Your job is to translate the language of the body into verbal language. You are tracking two qualities: muscle tension and energy. In this second step, you describe *how the tension and energy feel* in your body. Your body is speaking to you with twinges and tightening and pressure and wants to know you get the message.

You may be tempted to skip through this step, but it serves a specific purpose: to foster a connection between the part of yourself *having* the experience and the part of yourself *observing* it. It brings reflective consciousness to what has been an unconscious sense in the body. This is the "how-to" at the heart of soothing unrest.

Perceiving sensations and *naming* sensations with words activate different areas of your brain. Interoception lets you "hear" what your heart and muscles and lungs are saying. As you attune to what you feel inside, nonverbal parts of your brain that sit between the cortex and the mid-brain, such as the thalamus and insular cortex, activate and gather data. When you put those preverbal experiences into words, you activate higher regions of the brain that process language. This is the beginning of a reflective process. You are coming into relationship with what is happening inside you. This step is like when you *actively* listen to someone, rather than just wait for your opportunity to say your piece.

Go back to *where* you feel unrest and now say the word for that place. Then name *what that unrest feels like* in each location. Feel it and put it into words. "My shoulders are hunched" or "My neck is tense" or "My jaw is clenched" or "My calves are tight." The most common descriptors of tension are *tense*, *tight*, or *pressure*. To describe energy people often say they feel *agitated*, *fidgety*, or *jumpy*. What follows are some examples of other words you can use to describe what your unrest feels like.

Words for Tension

- aching
- bloated
- bracing
- choking
- compressed
- constricted
- cramped
- crunched
- crushing
- frozen
- hard
- heavy
- hollow
- knotted
- limp
- pinched
- pulled in
- rigid
- spasm
- squeezed
- stiff
- strained
- stretched
- stuck
- taut
- thick
- tight
- weighted

Words for Energy

- agitated
- buzzing
- churning
- draining out
- electrical
- fidgety
- fluttery
- humming
- jittery

- jolting
- jumpy
- prickly
- pulsing
- quivering
- radiating
- rising up
- shivering
- surging

- swirling
- tingling
- trembly
- twitchy
- vibrating
- whirling
- wobbling

Observe (Investing in Yourself)

The first two steps let you notice what you feel, but now you must slow down and "pay attention." Noticing is necessary: you can't pay attention to something you haven't noticed. But paying attention deepens your noticing into an *experience* of what you feel. "Paying" is a perfect verb for this step. Think of paying attention like paying money: you are *investing in yourself* in this step. You are spending time and energy and attention to fully experience unrest so you can open to emotion and grow.

With "observe," you *enter into* what unrest feels like. Here you *contact* the parts of your body that are communicating with you. Imagine yourself gently leaning on the discomfort, bending toward the places that do not feel good right now. Nuzzle up against them like a horse against a familiar hand. Breathe warm interest and care into the tension.

Ask, "What does that feel like?" over and over, using the answer from the prior question as the start for the next one:

What does *tense* feel like in my shoulders?
It feels like a turtle shell.

What does *turtle shell* feel like?
It feels like hunching.
What does *hunching* feel like?
It feels like a burning in my trapezius muscles.
What does *burning* feel like?
It feels hot and tight and tired.
And what does *that* feel like?
Achy.
What does *achy* feel like?
Like a deep throbbing feeling.

Your body will soon feel your genuine interest and know it is safe. It will release, loosening and softening and letting you in.

This step is not all-or-nothing, and even a small decrease in tension is plenty. The body rarely gives full release, and in chronically tense areas, not much might change. But if you notice 20 percent less tension in an area, it means your body has registered your attention and understands there is no external danger. Like a soldier who has been given the order to "stand down," your body will be relieved of its need to protect you and will drop its guard.

The Sigh

When your body registers your attention, you may involuntarily sigh. Notice your sigh! It is easy to ignore it or think to yourself that you "took" that breath yourself but be advised: that sigh is a wonderful gift from your unconscious self. It is letting you know your unrest has been soothed and the door to a deeper level of yourself is opening and allowing emotion through. You will want to learn to look for and treasure that signal, because it lets you know right in that moment that the spike is down, and emotion can flow.

WIN, with Warmth, Interest, and Nonjudgment

How you pay attention to unrest is key to your success in soothing it. You are a heliotrope; you grow toward warmth and light. As from the sun, warmth and light can radiate from your consciousness toward yourself, encouraging you to emerge and grow. *Warmth. Interest. Nonjudgment.* These three qualities of attention are so important. I want you to think of them as the way you will "win" in soothing unrest and fostering your growth.

Warmth

Warmth opens us. It is gentle and engaging. It melts and softens the hard edges of things.

Warmth is the same look new lovers give each other as they are in the throes of falling in love. There is a delicacy in the attuned attention they give to one another. But warmth is not only present for new lovers. You can hear warmth in round tones in the music of your voice where you feel love or care. You see it in body language as you form shapes that curve toward another, matching them in rhythms and gestures. Warmth is there when you feel wanted and seen by another.

Can you imagine feeling that way toward yourself? Even when you are triggered with unrest? Can you hear the warmth in the sound of your inner voice as you speak to yourself, as you invite your body to share what it feels?

Interest

Interest is the opposite of ignoring, suppressing, or turning a blind eye. Interest is not neutral. It is not a removed, clinical, dispassionate inquiry. Nor is interest fretful, looking for where the disaster is likely to be hiding. Interest is *leaning* toward yourself, like the friend who says, "No, *really*, how are you?" Not content to accept the superficial "fine," interest solicits us to go deeper. Interest is deciding that you *want* to know what the unrest feels like. It is a willingness to know the details, the subtleties of the experience. The message to yourself is: "It matters to me what is going on in there." It is an *invitation* to the part of you feeling unrest to come forward and reveal itself.

"What does that *feel* like?" As you ask this question over and over, more layers are revealed. A natural function of attention is that the more you notice, the more you notice. More detail emerges, affirming you are truly paying attention. Be curious about everything that surfaces.

Explore your internal experience like a traveler to a new land, where you need to observe the customs and not assume what things are and what they mean. Whisper the inviting words "tell me more" as your body opens to you and lean in closer. Ask again. Let your body know you want to know everything it feels.

Nonjudgment

Judgment evokes shame, and shame shuts everything down. As I was writing this section, I was tortured with negative judgments. I saw mocking eyes reflecting the acronyms I DO and WIN. I heard a critical voice tell me how silly this all is. And I was stuck for a while.

Blessedly for me, a friend called asking how my writing was going. I told her how lame and boring and silly it was and how I'd lost the thread. She nonjudgmentally noted my judgment, and suddenly I saw what I wanted to say. She created safety so I could see my judgment, reminding me to *be with* myself there to become unstuck. The fact is, I *am* goofy. My clients will tell you that after a difficult piece of work, I might come up with a silly accent or quirky angle that makes us laugh, blasting us to the next place we need to go. That's just me. And just being me, and revealing me, is vulnerable. I got blocked and wanted to hide, and I was fortunate to be drawn out of hiding by the acceptance of my friend.

We spend far too much time *being less* by judging ourselves to avoid *being lessened* by someone else's judgment. But we rob the world of the gift of our fullest expression. You deserve to accept yourself in your vulnerability. But if you do not, you can locate a nonjudgmental pair of eyes within, looking back at you. It doesn't matter if just a moment ago you were judging yourself; just move to the next level of awareness, see your judgmental feelings, and accept yourself there. Like a set of stacking Russian dolls, your consciousness holds you in ever-larger circles.

Nonjudgment does not mean being without discretion. It's not being so open-minded that your brains fall right out of your head. It is not simply saying, "Oh, that's just how it is; that's just how I am." It is removing the black/white, good/bad, either/or, and making room for the complex mixture of your experience. Nonjudgment says, "You are worth paying attention to" and makes it safe to be seen and to grow.

The Commitment to Living Vulnerably

I shared my life for nineteen years with a gorgeous guy. He was a Himalayan cat, a fluffy furball of love named Gizmo. One warm June day, when Gizmo was about ten years old, we were out in the garden with Phil, a dear eighty-year-old friend. Suddenly, Gizmo was engulfed in an inner electrical storm. His body was snapping and his limbs flailing as twisting spasms overcame him, and I looked on in helpless horror. I thought he might die. My heart was pounding, frantic with fear.

In that moment, Phil reached down with a big, gnarled hand and softly, gently, firmly laid it upon my sweet cat. Phil's calm, loving presence surrounded this jigging creature with light and warmth. And I could feel Phil's grounded holding of me in that moment as well.

Phil leaned toward the pain and uncertainty of what was happening. He did not deny anything about the seriousness of the seizure, nor pretend everything was fine. We did not yet know. But he held a space around the not-knowing. In his own body, he found a place of connection and he reached from there to link with us and anchor us. Gizmo's seizure went on for the longest minutes of my life. At the end he was exhausted and disoriented, his fluffy little body slack and life-less. Then after some time he roused himself and, cradled in Phil's arms, came back to the world.

Phil held both Gizmo and me in our distress. And in doing so, he not only soothed us but also gifted me with an experience that grew me. I learned that I was worth being with and caring about in the painful throes of vulnerability. I could feel an almost immediate strengthening of my own capacity to hold Gizmo and myself in the same way.

For close to ten years, Gizmo continued to be randomly overcome by violent convulsions. Again and again, I practiced leaning in and holding. I'd be torn awake in the night by his sudden contortions, my heart thumping like horses' hooves, and find myself in the place of "I can't." It was so scary and painful. Pushed up hard against the limits of my ability to stop the awful assault, I would feel part of me helpless and flailing and yearning for escape, while another part of me committed to soothing unrest and staying present. I did not detach. I did not shut down. I was not overwhelmed, despite intense pain. I breathed. I felt my own body with precision, aware of the urge to speed up and flee. I acknowledged that and instead I slowed down, feeling unrest until my body knew I was there.

Then I reached toward Gizmo and gently pressed my hands on his shaking frame. I tried to really feel his little body. It felt awful to me, and again, I wanted to fix it and make it all better. I honored myself in that urge and felt my chest tighten with an ache of sorrow. I accepted myself in the moment of my helplessness. I breathed even slower. I murmured softly as the jerking slowed. He sensed me there and eventually (it felt like forever) stilled. I wiped the drool from his ruff and lay with him until he was back. And we came through it another time. There was nothing I could *do*, but there was something I could *be*. I could be present.

Gizmo and Phil both crossed the rainbow bridge many years ago, but they live on in my heart and mind in so many ways. I learned what it takes to commit to living vulnerably: leaning toward when everything inside screams to run away, and grounding into the body with warm interest and nonjudgment.

Love Defined: The "WIN"

Warmth, interest, and nonjudgment are the "how to," of paying attention to unrest, which is also the "how to" of *loving*. They interweave and form a holding environment of safety and connection. You need all three together. If you only have two, for example, warmth and interest, you want to open up, but if you are judged you need to shut back down. Warmth and nonjudgment without interest are like a ditzy friend who is nice but not present, whose lack of interest makes you feel unseen. And interest and nonjudgment without warmth makes you feel like a clinical project, something examined under a microscope. And who wants to expose themselves then?

How you approach your unrest, emotions, the people you love, and the world itself is the key to your quality of life. Your approach to life *is* your success; it's how you win. People come to me for help with a wide range of problems, but these all boil down to a single core issue: difficulty in loving or being loved. We feel loved when we feel we matter; others feel loved when they feel they matter to us. And when we are met and meet the world with warmth, interest, and nonjudgment, we win.

Staying On Track as You Track Yourself

How can you tell whether you are tracking yourself precisely? What are the signs that you are "on track" or "off track"? There are four clues: *fluctuation*, *safeness*, *compassion*, and *complexity*.

Fluctuation

If, as you pay attention, you feel no change in your unrest, you have the first clue you are off track. The body is constantly shifting, sometimes obviously and other times subtly. If you check in and say to yourself, "The tension feels exactly the same as it did a moment ago, there is no difference in intensity or quality at all," then you know you have not dropped down deep enough or gone slowly enough or leaned in closely enough to register what is happening inside.

Your body may not release tension as soon as you pay attention, but something may still be happening. You must go very slowly to drop down into the *experience* of unrest, rather than stay up in the *idea* of unrest. Even when you pay attention to chronically tense places in your body, you will feel small pulses or tingles or quivers as you stay there with precision. And the quality of the sensation changes: its intensity may go up or down, it may spread or shrink in size, or the location may change.

Safeness

Another clue that you are on track is a feeling of being a bit safer. Do you feel a release of tension, no matter how slight? Do you feel more spacious, or softer? When the body registers your attention, it knows there is no external danger and muscle tension lessens, agitation diminishes. This sense of safeness is not all-or-nothing; even a small shift counts.

I've sat across from more folks than I can count who've assured me this slow focus on body experience is a waste of time. Until, that is, they do the work of being in their bodies. Then it becomes palpably clear that the *concept* of being safe is hugely different from the *felt sense* of being safe. The mind's idea of safety does not shift things. This is one reason it is difficult for people to improve their lives by simply reading self-help books. Cognitive information shifts our ideas about things, but real transformation arises out of our experience of these things. That takes being in the body. And that takes time.

Compassion

The third sign you are on track is compassion toward yourself in what you are doing and feeling. If you feel you are not doing this "right," are impatient with the feelings of unrest, or like you shouldn't need to pay attention, you are off track.

"What's the big deal?"
"So what if it's tight? It's always tight."
"I probably overused it earlier today."
"What a waste of time."
"This is just navel-gazing."

These judgments can become big obstacles. We'll soon spend some time on how to address them, but for now noticing when you lack compassion is good. When you're on track, you care about yourself. You feel patient and kind toward yourself. You matter, even if what you feel does not feel good.

Complexity

Complexity is being aware of multiple aspects. You are a multidimensional being with a mixture of inner experiences shifting and dancing and rising and falling. Even in my happiest moment, I live with a trace of sadness that my happiness won't last forever...

Complexity involves experiencing your inner "four-ring circus": *motivation, resistance, observation*, and *choosing*. Each of these aspects is an experience, which means it "feels" like something in the body.

Motivation feels like being pulled forward. It is drive, being willing to do whatever it takes to foster your growth, despite discomfort. Notice the physical energy of this feeling propelling you forward to stay with the work of paying attention to unrest.

Resistance feels like bracing. It is the natural discomfort in staying with yourself when you don't feel good. Notice if you feel shame (like there is something wrong with you), guilt (like you are doing something wrong), or threat (like something bad will happen if you stay focused on yourself). These reactions are normal when you experience unrest, and they produce a physical experience of bracing against.

Observation feels like differentiation. You are the observer. As you pay attention to unrest, do you notice yourself witnessing it? Can you sense yourself as *separate from* and also being with what is happening in your body?

Choosing feels like freedom. You are the chooser. You do not choose to have unrest but whether you embrace it or fight it is up to you. Can you notice what the choice feels like, either way? This is a *feeling of freedom*, like there is more space for you. You are equally worth caring about no matter what you choose. What does knowing that feel like to you?

Obstacles to Answering Your Call

As you experience the feeling of vulnerability in your body, you will face obstacles. You need to go slowly enough. You need to trust that what goes up will come down. You need to rehabilitate your idea of what it means to be selfish. And you need to differentiate anxiety from unrest, and then block anxiety's source.

Going Too Fast

If you rush, you cannot soothe unrest. You can only soothe your body at the body's pace.

I was bewildered in my early days as a psychologist when I would mirror patients' emotional states back to them only to be met with a blank look. I was surprised because my "empathy meter" is generally above average—I'm used to being fairly accurate in my best guess at another's internal state (of course, not always, and I regularly check to confirm my hypotheses).

When I presented this in supervision with a senior clinician, she instructed me to wait a full two or three seconds *after* I picked up the information before mirroring it back. The delay made a remarkable difference. I was perceiving the client's subtle bodily shifts in blood flow, muscle tension, pupil dilation, breathing, and so on, and was sending back my integrated sense of that information (as in "so painful" or "so sad") before the client had registered the experience. The reaction was in the client's body and on their face *before* it was in their awareness. When I took that extra bit of time, the results were amazing. Clients received my feedback as validating rather than confusing.

Your body knows before you know. The body is fast. Emotional truth is there in your physiology before it reaches your conscious knowing. That is what we mean when we speak of unconscious signals from the body. But once you are aware of unrest and want to intervene with your conscious mind, once you have the "idea" that you will soothe unrest, your conscious mind thinks it should have done so already. Conscious thought is nimble and quick: "I think it, and it is so." But the body needs to feel your presence in order to know it is safe, and that interoceptive process takes time.

You need to slow your awareness as much as you possibly can, and then go at least five times slower than that! To help you slow down, visualize something that moves glacially slow. Have you ever done tai chi? Or watched someone performing a tai chi sequence? There is no rush, no hurry, just a focused steady flow of hands pushing energy through the air. Or have you ever taken the time to watch a snail just steadily go from point A to point B? Feel how slow that is. Or visualize opening a box of molasses, thick and cold from the fridge, and imagine it oozing into a bowl. Or picture an ice cube sitting on your kitchen counter, melting in real time.

If you hurry through this process, you'll get a superficial sense of your body, but your body will not feel *your* presence. Further, when you hurry, you reenact an old movie, one in which what you feel doesn't really matter. You send yourself the message that you are not really worthy of warmth and interest and patience. And it is time for *that* movie to end.

Fear of Overwhelm

When you bring full attention to the felt sense of unrest, it typically subsides. But sometimes when you focus inside, your sensations intensify. When you have ignored unrest for a long time and then suddenly give it attention, it can temporarily amplify. You may feel an unexpected rush of emotion that is distorted by the high level of unrest. If you're not prepared for this, what is going on inside may feel like "too much" and as though something is wrong. Prepare yourself with the thought that your unrest may indeed spike higher when you first tune in, and plan to anchor your attention even more fully and lean toward what you feel with even more warm interest. All your body needs to know is that there is no immediate physical threat, and your sustained nonjudgmental attention is the evidence of safety your body is looking for.

Fear of being overwhelmed runs deep. And for many of us, this fear holds a kernel of truth, because we may have been, or may have seen someone else, overwhelmed in the past. But we are never overwhelmed by emotion alone. Unregulated unrest makes emotional experience feel like too much. When unrest is soothed, our emotion, despite its intensity, feels healing. Have faith that what goes up will come down.

Not Being Selfish (Enough)

Does focusing attention on your inner experience feel indulgent? Perhaps you tell yourself that you shouldn't be so full of yourself? Yet who or what *else* would you want to be full of? Or would you want to be *empty* of yourself?

You can only truly give from fullness. If you are neglected or depleted or underdeveloped, that is the reservoir from which you give. Like a raincloud, you must be full before you can shower your gifts upon others and the world. Trying to give from emptiness creates a terrible vacuum, a sucking force that demands to be repaid. The resentment builds until it forms lightning bolts that can strike without warning. Taking care of yourself is your first priority. You need to listen to messages that ask for rest, exercise, nutrition, space, quietude, closeness, meaningful work, and joyous play.

So often we wish to be larger than we are, to need less than we do. We sublimate our needs to minimize conflict, or to win approval or love. Yet a need by definition is something essential, *of our essence*. Intrinsic and indispensable to who we are.

In denying your need, you deny your basic self. In filling your needs, you fill yourself. And when full, you naturally and organically will feel the need to give from that fullness. And so selfishness may not be so selfish in the end…

Scary Stories and Nasty Movies

Worry and self-criticism are the first things to look out for if unrest isn't coming down with attention. You can't soothe unrest if menacing, bullying stories are running in the background of your mind. These cognitive mechanisms evoke anxiety, which has the same physiology as unrest but is generated moment by moment from the lies you are telling yourself. Those threats take your focus out of the living moment to another place and time, and no amount of attempted body awareness will soothe unrest from there. It is not enough to mindfully observe these thoughts; blocking them is key to getting yourself home in your body in the present moment. These thoughts are defensive processes. We will look at how to recognize and deactivate them in chapter seven.

PRACTICE: ANSWER YOUR CALL. SAY, "I DO"

Think of a vulnerable situation in your life, something you wish you had more control over, or wish was different. Maybe your big sister cannot let go of her "big" status even though you're both in your forties now. Or your ever-so-helpful coworker cannot stop looking over your shoulder to let you know how much better he would do your job.

When the situation is clear in your mind, turn on your phone's video function. Speak directly into the camera and record yourself describing the situation. Make sure you are shooting the video at a distance so your whole torso is in view while you squarely face the camera. Describe the issue in enough detail to identify what is hard for you. Focus on what exactly makes this situation vulnerable and describe how it affects you. Say aloud how important this is for you, and what it would mean for it *not* to be sorted out.

When you are done, pause the video. Take a moment to look at your surroundings and assure yourself that in this moment there is no threat to life and limb. Some feelings may be stirring, but notice there is no real danger. Think about being warm toward your vulnerable self. Feel genuinely interested in learning more about you. And commit to being nonjudgmental, accepting yourself no matter what you uncover.

Now, play back the video of yourself, and with warmth, interest, and nonjudgment go through the steps: identify, describe, and observe yourself as you watch the video:

1   Identify where in the body you can see or recall feeling tension or agitation. Make sure you cover the whole body from head to toe.

2   Describe what the tension and agitation feel like. This means coming up with adjectives (refer to the lists on page 137 if you get stuck).

3   Observe yourself. Go slow and ask yourself, "And what does *that* feel like?" inviting deeper levels of awareness until you sense your body has registered your attention.

Look for markers of being on track, such as fluctuations in your bodily arousal, feelings of safeness as you tune in, a sense of compassion for yourself, and awareness of your complexity, including wanting to know more about yourself, resistance, differentiating from your sensations, and being able to choose to approach or avoid what you feel. Also notice if you get stuck and see if you can observe what might be blocking you, like going too fast or judging yourself.

Bravo! Taking time to be this curious about your inner felt experience is success! We normally ignore and push through and solve problems without connecting with what the truth feels like inside. As you give yourself the gift of your undivided attention, you send a message to the deepest places in you, saying, "I matter." From that place, you can begin to clarify who and what else matters to you, including others in your life and the larger world.

7

riding the wave
of emotion

*"'Free' is not free from feelings, but free to feel each one
and let it move on, unafraid of the movement of life."*

JACK KORNFIELD

RODRIGO WANTED deeper friendships. A college
mathematics professor who was successful in his
career and happily married with adult children,
Rodrigo felt "less than" others, especially with men
he wanted to befriend. He habitually second-guessed himself,
editing his thoughts and feelings to avoid judgment or conflict. Although that made him successful at avoiding conflict,
it also made him very difficult to get close to. Over time, even
folks who seemed to like him would drift away.

This mystified Rodrigo. Anyone who met him found him
warm, intelligent, and thoughtful. There was no *reason* to feel
he couldn't be himself with others and, being such a reason-
able person, Rodrigo was at his wits' end when he came to
therapy, feeling lonely and not good enough.

We began therapy assessing his connection to his body as we tracked unrest. Our first efforts were challenging, as Rodrigo had lived in his head for a long time. His first words in answer to the question "What do you feel in your body?" were, "I think…" as he began analyzing before having any sense of how his body felt. Rodrigo "knew" he had feelings; he just stepped out of them so quickly that he didn't register them in his body. He said he found his feelings a bit threatening, "I'd rather not spend too much time in there. I don't like what it feels like."

Do you sometimes wish you felt more, or less, or differently? Of course you do. Emotion is a force of its own, flowing through you in rivulets and streams and oceanic breakers. Lifted by joy, fired up by anger, wracked with grief, quaking with fear, tugged by longing, roiling with guilt—when you open to emotion, you feel how your body is moved, and you know yourself as acted upon, not the actor. The word "emotion" is derived from words that literally mean movement: the French *émouvoir,* which means "to stir up," and the Latin *emovere,* meaning "to move outward." You need to be stirred and moved by your experience. As you are *moved by* emotion, you can be *moved to* your authentic self. Emotion is *how* reality touches you, reveals you, and transforms you.

Emotion is vulnerable and that vulnerability is revealed in our language. To "be moved" is passive; you *allow* something rather than direct it. You open to *receive* an experience rather than going out and grabbing it. You are carried there rather than getting there on your own two feet. Yet it is precisely in your openhearted willingness to be surprised that you can break free from the straitjacket of your preconceived ideas about who you are.

Rodrigo braced as he shared an example about a colleague. "He was talking about his squash game, so I asked about his technique and when he started talking, I couldn't find a way to edge back into the conversation. I felt like he wasn't interested in what I had to say, and I started to feel competitive with him, and I just shut down."

"What are you aware of right now, in your body?" I asked him.

He replied, "I feel weak, and out of my league," his mind jumping to *interpreting* what he felt. I helped him see those words as judgments rather than physical experiences. I encouraged him to slow down so he could get underneath the labels and feel sensations in his body. As he focused inward, Rodrigo felt his biceps tighten and his breathing shallow. He noticed he was pushing his toes into the floor, saying, "I'm ready to run." He shook his head, confused, and said, "I'm so feeble."

I invited Rodrigo to observe how judging himself prevented feeling in his body. He blocked his criticism and went back to tracking unrest until it began to ebb. Despite his discomfort and the pull of "not being good enough," Rodrigo stayed with the muscle tension. He cycled back and forth between his judgment and his curiosity about what was happening. With each attempt he managed to stay with his sensations a bit longer, and his unrest waned. By the end of that first session, Rodrigo was surprised: "I feel like I matter." Our careful, nonjudgmental attention to his physical experience gave Rodrigo a new sense of being okay just as he is. Even though nothing had changed in the outside world, Rodrigo felt better by mattering in his body.

Over the next sessions, Rodrigo deepened his practice of noticing and regulating unrest, and he understood in more detail what happened with prospective friends. Rodrigo saw his self-doubt rise whenever he wanted to reveal himself, change the subject, or disagree. "He'll think I don't know what I'm talking about." When I asked for evidence that people judge him, Rodrigo was perplexed, as there was none.

"Is it possible the judgment is coming from inside you, from the part of you that is critical toward yourself?" I inquired. He knew he could be hard on himself sometimes and was open to considering this possibility.

We continued to look at the same example of his colleague's squash game chatter, and as Rodrigo's shoulders squared and his breathing deepened, I asked what he was feeling toward his colleague. "Nothing," Rodrigo replied, despite clenched hands and gritted teeth. We persisted and after several tries Rodrigo saw he was angry. His anger didn't make sense to him, so he struggled to see it. I invited Rodrigo to feel the anger in his body. "You mean *physically*?" Rodrigo asked, as though this were the weirdest thing he'd ever been asked to do.

"Yes, physically," I said.

He tuned in to the feeling of anger and was surprised at how powerful it felt. He questioned and minimized his feeling. "The other guy didn't do anything wrong, I just *felt* judged. I've got nothing to be mad about. I shouldn't feel this way."

We continued to investigate Rodrigo's anger, and he was shocked as it rose. He was much angrier than he had realized, more than the situation warranted. He knew this and it made no sense to him. But as we stayed with it, something suddenly shifted and he sat up straight and leaned forward: "I have an image of my older brother right now."

I asked him to tell me what he saw. "He's towering over me and calling me useless and stupid. He's pushing me in the chest and shoving me down. Then he has his knee on my chest and he's spitting on me. I can't get up and he's laughing. I feel so small and I can't stop him."

"When you welcome your emotions as teachers, every emotion brings good news, even the ones that are painful."

GARY ZUKAV

Rodrigo was breathing heavily, his fists clenched, his feet planted firmly on the floor. "My god, that is so long ago. I haven't thought of this memory for decades," he said. In that moment Rodrigo recalled how his brother had taunted him for much of his childhood. His parents ignored it and acted like it was just "boys being boys," no one realizing the harm it was doing to Rodrigo's self-esteem.

In subsequent sessions, Rodrigo was able to soothe unrest and ride waves of deep anger and grief as he faced his brother's years-long abuse. He had blamed himself for being weak and not worthy of respect from his brother, nor protection from his parents. A deep sense of loss arose as he realized how he had longed for his brother's approval, and had always loved him despite the abuse.

Rodrigo relived and worked through deep rage and sorrow. This was painful but released layers of tension from deep inside him. The battle about his worth was over. By the time we finished our work together, Rodrigo had spoken with his brother about what had happened and received a beautiful apology. He became more assertive, including with men he admired, and no longer silenced himself. He stopped avoiding conflict and let others know and connect with him more deeply.

Rodrigo described, in our last appointment, how he had transformed from accessing deep emotion. "I don't berate myself anymore. I'm having feelings and I'm taking care of them. And they take care of me! I don't feel 'less than' anymore."

The Gifts of Emotions

Emotions give you energy, information, and meaning. Core emotion changes your bodily state, first disrupting you and then increasing your sense of aliveness. Emotion *motivates* you, drawing you into or away from situations and people and things. It fosters access to blocked resources and capacities and can unlock information previously held in coded forms, such as dreams or disconnected memory fragments. It allows you to feel *empathy*, to understand the interior of others and connect with them. It releases tendencies to act, physical urges that energize you and direct your behavior.

Tapping into your emotions can expand your sense of mastery and competence. You feel more in touch with your true self. Emotion underpins resilience, the ability to bounce back from difficulty. And emotion is *integrative*, linking body, mind, and spirit through the biochemistry and physiology and felt sense of our feelings.

At the end of a wave of core emotion, a client once said to me, "All the atoms of me that were scattered have come back home. I've joined forces and I'm coming together with myself. I fill myself. I'm no longer divided. It makes me feel like I can handle things, like I'm safe. And it makes me feel more *me*."

Emotion tells you what matters to you, how it matters to you, and gives you energy to do something about it. *Emotion propels your growth, and unrest is the signal that emotion is stirring.*

Authenticity

We looked closely at authenticity in chapter four when we examined what you are growing when you soothe unrest and feel emotion, so we will just have a quick review here. Whether triggered from within your inner world of thoughts, sensations, and memories, or from your reactions to your outer world, emotions reveal you in your complexity and at your essence. Your emotional reaction reflects your history, temperament, capacities, innate inclinations, and current state. Your reaction also speaks of your appraisal and understanding. All these interwoven aspects of you filter incoming stimuli (the smell of melting chocolate, the news of a school shooting, the soaring strings of a symphony, the warm arms of your partner wrapped safely around you, the sight of a fallen bird, the peal of your infant's delighted laughter) and produce your unique, genuine experience of being.

Emotion gives you the most vital information about your true self. You can see this in children as they begin to tune in to and exercise this knowledge. If they are safe and mirrored accurately, children naturally develop a sense of themselves through their emotional reactions. They approach what feels good and avoid what does not: "I like the smell of freshly cut grass. I don't like brussels sprouts. I'm not interested in the evening news. I really, really like my cuddly toy dachshund that holds my pajamas." This embodied connection provides a solid base of self-knowledge from which to explore the world and emerge spontaneous and confident.

When you can fully feel what you feel, you feel like yourself. The truth of who you are comes alive as you are moved by emotion. The emergence of the real you is the greatest gift of being able to face and feel emotion.

Motivation

Emotion motivates you. It points you in the right direction and gives you the energy to get there. This is the *emovere* of emotion: energy becoming behavior. All your best efforts cannot succeed if they come only from your intellect. You can have an *insight* into what you need to do. You can analyze your way to a goal or a path. You can even begin the journey from the place of will. But to sustain your efforts you need to draw on the true power source that is emotion.

After six failed attempts on her own, Karen came to see me about her failure to manage her finances better. Time after time, she had created a budget and resolved to stick to it, only to find herself lured by some sexy new shoes or conned by a great "deal" or saddled with an unexpected repair that would break the bank, yet again.

Karen was an only child, and her single mother had raised her in a financially chaotic environment. Karen's maternal grandmother had kept Karen's mother on a tight financial leash. When Karen's grandmother died, Karen's mother inherited a fair bit of money that she quickly blew through, rebelling against her earlier financial restraints. Whenever her mother got hold of money, she spent like there was no tomorrow, but other times there wasn't enough for Karen's lunch or sports equipment or new jeans. The mixed messages were confusing and scary for Karen and made her unsure of herself. Karen came to feel she needed *things* to feel safe, and so began her journey into debt.

All this was clear to Karen when she came through my door. We did not have an "aha" moment together regarding the driving forces behind her money struggles. Her problem wasn't a lack of understanding; it was that she thought understanding alone would be enough to keep her on track. Understanding works fine as long as there is no stress, emotion, or unrest. But as soon as she felt vulnerable, as soon as she was faced with frustrations or hurt feelings, Karen would try to spend her way out of her discomfort.

Karen needed to *feel* what all of this meant to her in her body. I asked her to look closely for a trigger that may have stirred feelings for her the day before our appointment, when she'd gone online and spent triple her budget on a new purse. Karen had trouble identifying anything. I probed until she recalled she had been frustrated when her boss (a micromanager) had interrupted her in a meeting and questioned one of her decisions. Karen reported handling the interaction well. When I asked what had happened with her frustration, she said she had not felt any, but her hands began to fidget.

I invited her to tune in to her unrest. Karen described agitation and tension and stayed with the sensations until the unrest began to come down. She said her boss was hard to predict, that some days she would be easy to please and other times acted like nothing would satisfy her. As we slowed down and investigated the feeling more closely, Karen recalled feeling ashamed in front of her colleagues. Her face flushed and her brow furrowed as she declared, "It makes me feel so unsure when she does that to me!" I asked her if that was familiar and she immediately said, "Absolutely. I never knew how things were going to go with my mother... sometimes I could have anything I wanted, and then other times she made me feel so bad for asking for a new pair of shoes."

I invited Karen to stay with the anger. She leaned forward and karate chopped one hand onto the palm of the other as she said, "She should have cared how all that chaos affected me. It was so scary and confusing, and I had nowhere to turn." Just at that moment she looked down and noticed my boots. "Wow, those are great," she said. "Where did you buy them?"

That was the "aha" moment Karen needed. The neglected internal *feeling* of anger propelled her urge to spend money. Her automatic reflex kicked in right under our noses. She saw how, when anger rises and unrest stirs, she escapes from discomfort by looking toward "stuff" to distract her. I wiggled my foot and we both laughed. We practiced evoking the anger, soothing the unrest, and feeling the emotion all the way to the end of the wave. Each time she experienced the feelings, Karen grew stronger and clearer inside herself. She grew her capacity to bear her feelings, and over time no longer needed to spend herself away from her truth.

Rather than using willpower to avoid her urge to spend, Karen tamed the urge itself by feeling her feelings. She harnessed her desire for financial freedom and stability, and followed through on her commitment to be mindful about spending. She asserted herself when friends invited her to restaurants or when she felt tempted by a shiny new object on sale. Her power to stick with her plan came from her connection to herself in the truth of her feelings.

Insight shines a light on dreams and goals, and although it reveals your destination, it cannot take you there. Willpower can pry you out of old patterns, lifting your wheels out of a rut, but its energy burns out quickly. Emotion is the force that draws you steadily toward your goals. The fear of a life unlived, the anger at being robbed of your full self, the grief of lost time, the excitement of new possibilities, the joy at recognizing your emergent self—all these emotions impel you forward and sustain you on your journey.

Meaning

You are a meaning-making creature. A part of you is always at work, behind the scenes, making sense of your world and yourself. The meaning of your life originates inside you, from your emotional experience. Even more powerfully, research has demonstrated the intensity of your emotional experience contributes more to your sense of having lived a meaningful life than the positive or negative quality of what you feel. In other words, meaning is not enhanced by how "good" an experience feels but by *how deeply you are moved by it, good or bad.* Intense experience fosters greater self-reflection and more robustly shapes the narrative of your life. Paying inner attention to unrest when it heralds vulnerable emotion allows you to deepen and intensify your experience, enhancing the meaning of your life.

Meaninglessness is central to depression. Depression is not sadness; it is disconnection from what you feel. It is the emptiness that rushes in when you chronically suppress your feelings, saying, "It doesn't matter" over and over. When what you feel doesn't matter, eventually you don't matter. *And when you don't matter, nothing matters.* When a depressed person begins to feel sadness, when the tears are no longer just tears of frustration but become tears of grief and loss, this is progress. Sorrow is painful but it is also sharp and alive. You're no longer blunted, a walking zombie, a robot. From this place of feeling you can digest the meaning of your loss. It can matter. You can matter.

Emotional meaning is central to decision-making: when you do not know what you feel, you cannot decide. People with damage to the parts of the brain involved with emotion can still think, analyze, and talk; but when faced with a decision, they cannot meaningfully choose. They have lost the guideposts inside that tell them what is important. Imagine you are about to make a major decision, whether to quit your job or marry someone or move to a new country. You might list the pros and cons. How do you then decide? Do you simply add up the items on each side? Very unlikely. You would weigh each point using some system of value based on what matters to you, based on your feelings.

Understanding the meaning of interpersonal communication involves tracking nuances of emotion via body language. Your brain collects data—tone of voice, posture, facial expression, pupil size, blood flow to the face, and more—and filters it for signs of emotional significance. At the same time, your interoception system tracks your own internal reactions and uses them as additional feedback. Often, you're unaware of the influence of these cues unless they are absent, like with texting or emails. Emotional meaning is so important that we invented a new way to communicate online: the emoticon (a mash-up of "emotion" and "icon"). Emoticons are little illustrations that represent feelings, and the emoticon vocabulary has grown from a few basic glyphs denoting positive or negative feelings to hundreds of nuanced symbols. But even so, they are a thin gruel compared to the rich broth of embodied human relating.

This meaning-making gap became critically challenging during the COVID-19 pandemic, when everyone from grade-schoolers to grandmas had to connect on video platforms. "Zoom fatigue" entered our lexicon as, unable to access emotional cues, we became burned out by the increased cognitive load. Lack of true eye contact, the loss of fine-grained data with pixilation and delays, being trapped in a small visual field unable to move normally, and compensating with exaggerated facial expressions or big, weird thumbs-up gestures all created stress for our relational meaning-making. Zoom and other platforms did save a lot of us when meeting in person was not possible, but our brains had to work so much harder to make meaning when we could not simply be two bodies together.

When you try to make meaning of your life without considering your emotions, you are lost. Sketch out your life with intellect alone and you'll find the map doesn't match the territory. Your idea of who you are and your concept of what matters are not the truth of who you are and what matters. As you open yourself to be illuminated by emotion, the meaning of your life emerges like the world at dawn.

Empathy and Connection

The words "I hear you" said with genuine warmth can powerfully soothe distress. Your emotional capacities give you the strength to offer your presence and be accurately attuned in your support, rather than trying to "fix" the problem. When you do not need to harden against my pain, your open heart invites me to drop my defenses and face what I feel. When you validate me with "this is hard," I can access my inner strengths, and it becomes "not that hard." When your heartstrings resonate with mine, a song opens us both to a deeper truth. All these openhearted interactions hinge upon your ability to soothe unrest and tolerate the vulnerable waves of your emotion.

Your capacity to allow things to matter, sense the inner world of others, and be touched by others' feelings, is medicine our culture, our planet, and even your own body are crying out for. Empathy forms a foundation for your moral compass, directing you to care about wrongs and help those in need, including those close to you, disadvantaged groups, endangered animals, and the environment. Emotional empathy weaves you into the fabric of the larger world, fostering connections in which you support and are supported by others. Those who feel more connected to others have lower levels of anxiety and depression and higher levels of self-esteem. Your capacity to feel emotion generates a positive feedback loop of social, emotional, and physical well-being. Empathy and connection may save your life. Research has demonstrated that lack of social connection is a greater health risk than high blood pressure, smoking, or obesity. Strong connections increase longevity, strengthen immunity, and support faster recovery from illness. And taking care of and caring about the planet may save all our lives.

In this beautiful, cruel universe, where pain is inevitable, your bonds of connection forged of empathic resonance hold you, so you are not alone.

It Is Just a Feeling

When I began, many years ago, writing about the gifts of emotion for this book, I was going through a painful, post-divorce breakup. How piercing, how tender, and how raw it was. The ache inside was a bruise under my skin that covered my whole body. A cascade of chemicals in my brain was urgently signaling alarm, shock, sorrow, betrayal, and anger. I braced and tightened and held my breath against the pain. Thoughts arose to explain and escape the immediacy of my vulnerable feelings—thoughts that were themselves grievous and scary and painful. And triggered associations from long ago bubbled up, haunting me with bodily memories of earlier times I had felt alone and ashamed or overwhelmed.

Why would anyone stick with what this feels like? Why wouldn't any sane person shut down or seek an escape, a painkiller, or a sedative? That question is, of course, why I have been writing about the gifts of emotions. I am the pitchman for emotions, selling the value of feelings and being with them. I ask you to trust that crucial information, energy, and growth are to be had if you can just ride the waves.

In my own life, as for my clients, and as for you, the choice to face emotion is brave and difficult. It even seems a bit crazy to lean toward such pain and see it not as threat and harm but as healing and growth. But... then again, it is just a feeling. You know what I mean? Feelings are gold and they are just, you know, feelings. Feelings that need to be dealt with. And dealing with emotion means feeling emotion. The fruit of that labor is a deepened experience of being alive and yourself.

As I look back, I feel how "done" my old grief is, and how enriched I am for its transformational deluge having washed away unneeded elements within, revealing unexpected treasures. I chose to trust the process and love myself enough, in the face of steep spikes of unrest, to soothe my bracing body and ride waves of emotion through to the shore. My tsunami of pain tore deep channels for feeling, growing my confidence that I can face the truth and be okay. I gained access to how deeply I love, and recommitted to loving like that again, despite the risk of betrayal or loss. And not long after, when I had the good fortune to meet my loving, kind future husband, my heart was open and ready for love.

The Information and Energy of Core Emotions

Core emotions seem to be universally human. By the time you were four months old you could distinguish emotions in the faces of your caregivers, discriminating and responding in meaningful ways to others' emotions. The faces of anger, shame, sadness, fear, and joy are understood across many cultures. From remote tribes in New Guinea to city dwellers in North America, we reliably recognize facial photos of those "primary" emotions.

Yet even as emotion is a biologically rooted and shared human experience, your emotional signature is unique. Individual emotional reactions are shaped by temperament and personal history, and you discover them through paying close attention to your felt experience. It is time to learn the language of your own heart.

Six emotions to examine in detail are: sadness, anger, fear, guilt, shame, and joy. This examination is focused on healthy, core emotion. But, of course, there are also unhealthy, dysfunctional distortions of these emotions, which people may mistake for the real thing. In chapter eight we will look at defenses and the ways that people use pathological versions of emotions to avoid feeling the more painful truth of what they feel, such as compulsively motivated shame to cover anger.

Included are four prompts to familiarize you with broad commonalities, and then you can be curious how each uniquely moves you. What does it *feel* like? What is the *information*? What does it make you want to *do*? And what is the *gift*?

Sadness

Sadness and satiation come from the same Latin root, *satis*, which means "it is enough." When you feel sadness, you have stopped fighting with reality. ("No! I won't accept this." "It shouldn't be this way!" "If only...") Sadness is the place of "I can't." You surrender. You accept you cannot alter the outcome. It is what it is. Despite your desire, will, and best efforts, you are helpless to make things be the way you want. This can be a terribly painful and difficult place. There is a feeling of futility, as all your efforts not only *have* not and *will* not but *cannot* get you what you want. Sadness is integrative, as it acknowledges both your longing and the limits to making it so. Only from courageously inhabiting this place for as long as the waves rise and fall can we be delivered to renewed hope and purpose.

What does it feel like? Sadness feels like *moving inward*: energy rises up and then draws inward, like a leaf curling. It is as though you're in the fetal position as you focus on the deep internal work of understanding what has mattered to you, and accepting who you are now, without it. Sadness brings a loss of energy and a slowing of metabolism. You feel heaviness in the chest, tightness in the throat, pressure behind the eyes, and a prickling sensation in the nose. The outer corners of your mouth draw downward; your eyes are downcast. The inner corner of your eyebrows pulls upward, and the center of your forehead wrinkles slightly. Your shoulders sag, and you feel drained.

What is the information? The information in sadness is loss. Sadness informs you something matters to you that you cannot have. Sadness tells you that there is something you must let go, whether it is a person, a pet, a job, a dream, your health, the love of another, a cherished idea, or something else you might want or need but cannot control.

What does it make you want to do? The energy of sadness draws your attention inward to metabolize the loss. You are no longer interested in the goings-on of the external world. When people are in deep grief, they can be unaware, for example, that summer has passed until they notice the crunch of autumn leaves beneath their feet. Grieving is honoring the ways something has mattered to you. That's why you go over and over the details of what is gone as you reflect on the loss. You are reviewing the details so you can digest them, relinquishing what you must let go, and incorporating what remains.

What is the gift? Sadness is profoundly adaptive, moving you to come to terms with what cannot be changed instead of fighting reality or blaming yourself. Your tears are your resistance melting as you face and feel what you cannot have, so you can let it go and fully embrace what you do and can have. You are *reconstructing yourself* through this process. You come to a new understanding of who you are *without* this person or place or thing. And you realize you are resilient, will survive, and are still yourself.

Anger

When your boundaries are pushed, anger rises to push back and say no. Anger is the feeling of taking up one's rightful space. It energizes you to defend against intrusion and claim what is yours, including the right to be your authentic self. Anger is a powerful energy for correcting wrongs, whether in a relationship or in the larger world. Anger, like all emotion, varies along a continuum of intensity. At the low end of intensity, anger is simply assertion—the energy to express yourself, for example, to introduce yourself or disagree with others. As anger rises in intensity it can look like annoyance at being thwarted and can become full-blown anger at being violated.

What does it feel like? Anger feels like *pushing away*: an upward and outward movement of energy starts in your core, winding up through your chest into your throat. It is a hot, burning feeling like molten lava. There is an increase in nervous system activity, with adrenaline powering up your arms, hands, and legs. Your hands clench into fists, your feet press into the ground, and your shoulders and upper arms prepare to push. Your legs strengthen to assist in taking a stand and holding your ground. Your eyebrows lower and your lips narrow and tighten. You clench your jaw. Your tone of voice deepens and your eyes focus.

What is the information? Anger informs you that you need to push to take care of yourself: push outward with the arms and hands against some boundary violation, push down into the earth to take a stand, or push into the world to express yourself. That feeling may be a gentle nudge inside you to speak up in a social situation or to project yourself into the world in some way. Or it may be a more powerful surge rising up and saying that you need to stand and support yourself. In those situations, the feeling does not have the usual characteristics that we associate with anger, but rather it is the energy of *assertion* and is not directed at an external target. Assertion is the energy to risk putting yourself into the world. Self-expression is vulnerable, and assertion provides physical support for that risk.

In other situations, anger tells you about violation. It informs you that your boundaries have been crossed. It says you have been wronged, something has been taken from you, or you have been intruded upon. It can also speak to you of injustice done to others.

What does it make you want to do? Anger energizes you to correct a violation. You feel like defending or protecting. The feeling brings a connection to the powerful, hot core of you, grounding you with energy by activating your feet and legs. Your back strengthens and lengthens as your shoulders drop down and back. You have a backbone. You take up more space as your chest fills out and your arms and hands are energized to push. Many phrases reflect our intuitive understanding of the action tendency of anger: being "on solid ground" or "having solid footing," "taking a stand" and "putting your foot down."

What is the gift? Anger empowers you to fully express what is true for you, take a stand for what is right, correct a wrong, and protect yourself and others. Your anger helps you be taken seriously.

Fear

Fear helps you escape from immediate threat to life and limb. It focuses attention on the source of danger and mobilizes you to flee or fight. Fear tells you that you are not safe and must act to avoid being hurt or worse.

What does it feel like? Fear feels like *moving away*: It is sympathetic nervous system arousal. Adrenaline and other stress hormones put your body on alert. Your senses orient to the perceived location of the danger, trying to pick up information to determine how to best protect yourself. Blood moves away from the organs and the core toward the large muscles in your legs to mobilize you to run away. Your heart races and pounds harder, and your breathing is deeper and faster. Your eyes open wider and your eyebrows raise. You feel agitated and your body may tremble, especially the legs. Fear powers you up to fight or flee, and in that moment, you are stronger and faster than normal.

What is the information? Fear warns you that you are faced with an immediate threat to your safety (or to the safety of another). It tells you to act protectively, to escape whatever has triggered it. Fear hijacks all other feelings.

What does it make you want to do? Fear motivates you to flee from danger, to fight if you cannot flee, and to curl up and protect yourself (freeze) if you cannot flee or fight. There is an urgent focus on escaping the danger and moving toward safety. At the same time, fear directs your attention toward the threat, keeping your eyes and ears open to track it.

What is the gift? Fear gives you the power to rapidly mobilize, to identify the source of danger and protectively act to fight or escape.

Guilt

Guilt is relational. We only feel guilty because we care. Guilt is rooted in empathy. It speaks to you of your culpability when you have wronged another person, and it arises out of a loving drive to repair the wrong. For example, if you can allow yourself to feel the guilt of working too much and neglecting your loved ones, the pain of it can move you to prioritize taking more time for your family and friends. Guilt feels so bad that people will do almost anything to get away from it, yet the bad feeling is your friend. It feels so painful precisely because it wants to motivate you to relieve that unpleasant stimulus by facing your bad behavior and remedying it. Guilt, although it feels bad, is about your care for the other person's feelings and your desire to make things right.

What does it feel like? Guilt feels *heavy*: It is as though you are being weighted down and, at the same time, there is a gut-wrenching feeling of pain, like being punched in the solar plexus and having the wind knocked out of you.

What is the information? You have hurt someone, and it matters to you. As with all the emotions I am describing, this refers to *adaptive*, or healthy, guilt. There are defensive versions of guilt. For example, you may punish yourself with self-absorbed bad feelings of guilt as a substitute for engaging in the more painful work of repairing with the other person. Or, instead of feeling angry with a person who has wronged you, you might convert your anger into a self-attacking form of guilt to blame yourself for their behavior. These kinds of distortions are unhealthy guilt.

What does it make you want to do? Focus on the other person. Repair, confess, apologize, and resolve what was messed up inside you that made you do the crappy thing in the first place. Guilt underlies the courageous act of a true apology, where you acknowledge your transgression and take responsibility. This kind of apology takes you out of the equation. It is not the point that you didn't mean it or that you didn't have a bad intention or that you were tired or running late or you misunderstood or that you had a bad childhood. It is unequivocal. My bad.

What is the gift? Guilt leads to better relationships because you repair wrongs rather than ignore or smoothe them over. You show yourself to be a trustworthy and safe person who can be counted on to care when you cause hurt. Of course, sometimes the people you have wronged will not open themselves to your guilt and will not offer themselves to you to repair. Yet it is still a growth-promoting experience to feel your guilt because you can learn from your mistakes. You are only human and your experience of guilt links you to the rest of us flawed, mistake-making mortals. It fosters humility and interconnectedness. And it reminds you that you are a loving person.

Shame

Shame is meant to help you absorb the values of your community and engage with others based on a shared moral code. Although shame is portrayed almost exclusively in our current culture as something harmful, being "shameless" is not necessarily a good thing. One could argue that our political and corporate and religious leaders might benefit from a more rigorous dose of shame. Shame is different from the other emotions in that, rather than activating you, it lowers your arousal levels. Shame is an experience of inhibition. Shame motivates you to live up to your ideal self and prods you when your actions have fallen short of your own expectations. Shame is also about belonging; when you feel shame, you feel you are at risk of being "cut from the herd." We humans are profoundly social beings, and the risk of being ostracized is experienced as a devastating threat. When your expression of yourself is met with negativity or is ignored entirely, you feel shame. If you believe the reproach is warranted, your shame is a powerful force to adjust your actions. If you disagree with the judgment, the initial stab of shame is followed by anger, to correct the misunderstanding.

What does it feel like? Shame feels like *hiding*: The biology of shame involves a sudden shift from sympathetic to parasympathetic nervous system activity. Shame is a rapid downward drop in energy. Your heart rate slows, your blood pressure drops, and your breathing becomes shallower. You feel like hiding, being still and not seen. Your face flushes with heat and you have a sense of shrinking. You avert your eyes, and your face goes blank. You may bow your head forward. Your physical movement slows down.

What is the information? Shame tells you of your failure to behave in accordance with your own values. It is an uncomfortable but healthy cue that reins in your impulsivity or urges better care with the things and people and situations that matter to you. Shame prompts you to step up and do the hard thing you have been avoiding. Shame can also say you have been met with criticism, scorn, or impatience from others. This disfavor leads you to correct the disgrace. If the attack is abusive and a correction is impossible, you will feel anger at the injustice. If you have no outlet for your healthy anger, it may turn into pathological shame where you feel fundamentally unworthy, isolated, and alone.

What does it make you want to do? Shame puts the brakes on expression and exploration. It blocks spontaneous action. It makes you want to hide and shut down. You feel less vital. Your interest in the environment around you is reduced. But shame can remind you about your integrity, illuminating when you are not acting in accordance with your values. It can prompt you to step up and do better, leading to a renewed sense of integrity.

What is the gift? Shame helps you face up to behavior that falls beneath what you expect for yourself. Shame, because it is such a powerful down-regulator of energy, can aid parents in stopping a child's impulsive action, such as running into traffic or touching private parts in public. But shame must be immediately followed with reconnection and repair, so the child feels reunited. If there is no reconnection, the child will move from shame into humiliation, which is always a crushing, toxic experience. The key to helping another person in moving through shame is "eyeballs." Eye contact is essential for bringing another into connection again. The feeling of exposure and the impulse to hide are resolved with a warm, interested, and nonjudgmental gaze.

Joy

You are here for joy. That delight is your true purpose. No other duty is more important than allowing the radiance of joy to illuminate your being. And your being is the heart of this book. Unrest invites you into your experience of yourself as you are moved by the vulnerable force of emotion. When you are free to enter your experience, flowing with it all, even the pain, you meet your core self in a feeling of uplift and interconnectedness. Immersed in experience, joining with the inner currents of your awareness, you are astonished at the miracle of being consciousness in matter. You feel amazement that you could be here at all, that you can taste this strawberry, move your limbs in space, see the fluttering leaves on the maple tree, as in the delicious example animated in the Disney Pixar movie *Soul*. Joy emerges out of moments of harmony when you feel yourself as one soaring note in a glorious symphony. Joy is more than happiness or pleasure. It has a spiritual quality of shared communion even as it is intimately embodied and personal. When I read the experiences of people who have had psychedelic trips, I am struck by how similar those descriptions are to what I know of joy. It appears when the fretful ego is given a holiday, you can feel the soul singing under your skin.

What does it feel like? Joy feels like *moving toward*. It is expansiveness and openness. You feel "lifted up." C.S. Lewis describes joy thus: "It jumps under one's ribs and tickles down one's back and makes one forget meals and keeps one (delightedly) sleepless o' nights." Your chest feels open and enlarged, and your heart swells. A bubbly feeling fizzes in your chest. Your face lights up and your eyes shine. Your lips curve upward and your eyes crinkle at the corners. Joy maximizes positive excitement. There is increased activity in the brain center that inhibits sadness and anxiety. You feel more energetic and alive. You have a feeling of readiness, accompanied by a sense of inner calm.

What is the information? The information in joy is the feeling of "yes." It is the experience of engagement, the message that you are open to life in all the ways it presents to you. There is a sense of connection to something larger and at the same time of being precious in your small self. A close cousin of joy is healthy pride, the feeling of "I can do this" or "I did that." The feeling of pride and joy reinforces our openhearted willingness to invest all we have in showing up for life.

What does it make you want to do? Joy makes you want to reach toward what has evoked the feeling. It energizes you to approach and open to experience.

What is the gift? The gift of joy is delight in feeling more alive and intertwined with all life.

Emotional Flow: Let the River Run

Unrest spikes and disrupts you as it heralds a vulnerable rise of core emotion in your body. That flow of emotion may feel uncomfortable as it builds to a peak. Your capacity to ride the flow of feeling as it peaks and subsides is called emotional tolerance. When your tolerance is large, you have the deepest experience of emotion in your body while holding it in your reflective awareness. You have and hold.

If you visualize your emotional flow as a river, you can see how differently the water might run depending on the riverbank that holds it. If the bank is unstable and shallow, the water overwhelms the bank; this is having your emotional experience without holding it, and it feels like chaos. If the riverbank is constricted and narrow, it blocks the water; this is holding your experience without having it, and it feels like rigidity. If the riverbank is wide and deep, your feeling flows freely and yet is contained. You have the embodied experience of your feeling, and you hold it by reflecting on it with compassion. You are neither overwhelmed nor shut down and can truly benefit from the emotion's gifts. You feel deeply, delay impulses, and gain intimate knowledge of what is true for you.

Having without Holding: Chaos

Having without holding is chaotic. Your emotion is flowing, but the riverbanks are shallow. You ignore or catastrophize, unrest rather than regulate it with warm attention.

You lack the grounded, reflective awareness that would guide you to prioritize and soothe unrest so you can contain yourself in the welling up of emotion. Instead, unrest spikes too high while the wave of emotion rises, and you feel overwhelmed. You are flooded, unable to cope with the deluge.

This is the feeling of being "out of control." You feel like you are falling apart. You have a hard time concentrating or getting things done. You do or say impulsive things that you may regret later. You lose your temper or erupt into inappropriate tears or break into a panic attack. Inside you feel like the walls are falling down; there is nothing to hold on to. This feels so distressing that you think you need to avoid your emotions. To have an experience but be flooded by it is frightening. It feels awful for you and for the people around you. When you go through this or witness other people in this state, your own fear of feeling may be deeply reinforced. The loss of control seems a consequence of the size of the emotion itself.

Yet the problem is the riverbank, not the flow of emotion. The emotion is not too big; the riverbank is too shallow. The overwhelmed person is not paying attention to unrest to soothe the arousal. The ignored arousal stays high and mixes with the energy of emotion, amplifying and distorting its flow, and the riverbank overflows.

Not all expression of feeling is healthy; some eruptions let off steam but leave you feeling powerless. Feelings that overwhelm you while unrest is high are frightening and unproductive. You feel out of control and behave in impulsive ways with bad consequences. You need to grow a strong capacity to pay attention to unrest in the body, to contain the flow of emotion. Repeatedly soothing unrest is like sandbagging the riverbank, building it up until its sides are strong and you are confident that they will hold.

Holding without Having: Rigidity
The other end of the continuum of emotional regulation is rigidity. Your flow of emotion is narrowed to a trickle, and

you feel stuck. Unrest prompts an unconscious impulse in you to shut down, as though feelings are dangerous. Without realizing it, you avoid letting yourself be moved. But if you cannot be touched or moved, you cannot grow. Unlike people who are overwhelmed, excessively controlled people typically appear fine on the outside. You seem to be coping well, getting things done, but inside you have a sense of emptiness. Living like this is just going through the motions. You ignore or rein in what you feel, often by pushing your limits. You work excessively long hours or train for marathons or set perfectionistic standards. When things do not go according to plan, you might feel irritated until things can be put back where they belong.

But feelings continue to flow whether you pay attention to them or not, and pressure builds. At some point, feelings may break through, and when they do, they are intense and even harder to regulate. They may erupt—either exploding outward or imploding inward—giving further evidence that emotion is dangerous. This creates a vicious circle, where you commit to working harder at keeping your feelings down.

Again, the problem is not in the flow of emotion. That is always just right, as it is, inside you. The problem is the riverbank is so narrow that your awareness and experience of emotion are blocked, your expression curbed. You don't know that you are sad or joyful or angry or afraid, or if you do, you are not allowed to show it. When you shut down, life loses its richness and meaning. You may not feel motivated or take risks. On the other hand, you may adhere to discipline in a rote way that allows you to complete things. But you get little satisfaction in completing the job.

You need to feel what your closed-off holding does to you in the body: the bracing just beneath the barrier you have erected. Feeling the ache in your muscles or the clenching in your jaw opens you to letting your experience matter. Then you can come to know in your own experience that feeling emotion is vulnerable but not dangerous.

Having and Holding: Flow

In between these polarities of overwhelm and shutdown is the sweet spot where you grow capacities for authenticity, resilience, and connection. Here emotion flows and is contained. You prioritize unrest and pay attention to it with warm interest until your body knows it is safe and then allow the flow of emotion to move you. You bear the uncomfortable rise of feeling until it ebbs, and access a deeper truth of who you are.

James came in to see me looking to stop his inner ups and downs and get a "flat line" inside. He had struggled with anxiety and panic attacks for many years. He was wary of my focus on being in the body and connecting with emotion. He told me, "Sandra, you can put that box of tissues away for my appointments because you're never gonna see me cry. I'm not *that* kind of guy." I reminded James (with a wink) that "flat line" is a term used in the medical field to describe death, and I let him know I couldn't sign on for that as our goal.

James and I worked on his panic disorder and progressed well, helping him stay with himself during the rapid, dreadful rise of arousal as a panic episode occurred. He became aware of his body as it signaled to him before a panic attack, and he learned how to tune in and soothe his body with warm interest. He identified the scary stories that evoked anxiety and grew his capacity to block them and redirect to the reality and safety of the present moment. He rarely had full-blown panic attacks anymore. He didn't even worry about having them. He was no longer afraid of his fear. But he was still afraid of his sadness.

Then his sweet golden retriever puppy died suddenly. She was barely a year old. And James cried. He opened to his feelings of helplessness and felt the loss. He used the capacity for paying warm attention we had grown for resolving his panic, and found that he could both feel and deal, even in the face of his grief. He could accept himself in the vulnerability of being moved by his emotion. He didn't have to suck it up and pretend it did not matter. He could be carried to depths of his grief, lifted to joy and love, and moved by gratitude for the brief time he had with his pup.

James shared his loss with others. He knew some people might judge him as "weak" for having tears about "just a dog," but he didn't care. He deepened his humanity and felt greater empathy for others in their sorrow. And he really liked the man that he discovered in himself through fully experiencing his loss.

Afterward James said to me, "I don't want to be the kind of guy who doesn't get upset when his dog dies. And I don't want to be the kind of guy who's afraid of being broken by those feelings." James let go of his wish for a flat line and could experience the richness of his inner life. He became larger as a person, stronger as a man. *That* kind of guy.

Reaching the Shore, Reaching Your Core

At the end of a wave of core emotion, a feeling of aliveness fills the body. As one client told me, "It feels as though gravity has been flipped around and I'm lifted up." And that reversal of gravity shows on the face; the eyes look up, the corners of the lips turn up, the face seems to lift. Better than surgery, I joke to my clients, but it's not really a joke. People literally seem to lose years of struggle and strain after they've been carried by the tide of feeling to the shore. One client enthused, "What I intrinsically am *works*, is good." It is as though there is no more "work" to do. Now you can get out of the way and allow being to be enough.

As you feel your emotion through to its natural conclusion you come to your core. When people arrive here their words often have a poetic quality, as though everyday language is too blunt an instrument. They use images and metaphors to describe how they feel. "I am a bird, wings spread, soaring." "I'm a huge Redwood and a great stillness fills me." "An unquenchable fire burns inside me." Or they use very simple language: "I am whole." "I am utterly okay." People speak of feeling calm and confident and clear and capable. They feel connected.

This is the reward for all the hard work of staying with yourself, despite cultural messages extolling the virtues of stoicism, despite longstanding defenses, despite bumping up against implicit memories of being overwhelmed by emotion long ago, despite quivers of unrest, despite the sometimes-intense pain of emotion, and despite not being able to do it in one fell swoop and perfectly.

And it is glorious to witness. It never fails to move me when I am part of the emergence as another spirit bursts forth, embodied and luminous, more fully themselves. A shimmering energy emanates from the person and fills the space between us. We are both lifted up, and deeply grateful.

Just as you have a built-in protective urge to avoid or escape unrest, so too do you have a deep, intrinsic longing to reach toward your presence. On the other side of your wave of emotion, having soothed your body in its restless physiology and navigated those churning waters, you find a deeper, truer sense of who you are. Something fits in a new way inside and you feel more complete.

Often when I ask my clients how it feels on this new shore they reply, "It feels good." This is the essence of what they feel in this place—they *are* good there. It is what it is and it is okay. I am what I am and I am okay. They are not without residual pain or loss or anger or joy. But it is all good.

As one client said to me in a calm, deep, quiet voice, "I want this again."

PRACTICE: SURF YOUR WAVE OF EMOTION

Eventually, you will practice this by noticing emotion as it arises naturally in your day. But as a first step, think of a time in the past when you felt an emotion like sadness or joy or anger; or if that is too hard, watch a movie that evokes some emotion. Use your voice recorder on your phone and, when you notice the feeling rising, describe everything you can about how it moves you. Track it in your body. It is okay if the feeling does not make sense to you. Feelings always have an inner logic, but sometimes you cannot see it.

As you feel the emotion, visualize yourself on a surfboard riding the wave and tracking your body, relaxed yet strong. Your feet and legs are anchored, your core is taut, but you are hanging loose. You are connected to your body and focused on feeling the wave of emotion carrying you.

As the wave begins to peak, feel yourself tense up as you resist the experience. Then, rather than stiffen against and endure the experience of the wave of feeling, switch focus and feel the unrest in your body. Bring gentle awareness to the physical tension until it eases, and when your heart rate comes down a bit and your body settles, return to the emotion and ride the wave again. Describe how the emotion moves you, in your body. Do this over and over. Surf the wave of feeling, describing as you go, until you feel your body state shift from emotional activation to a calm feeling of clarity and connection. You have arrived at a new shore of yourself.

Once you are done, listen to your recording. Notice your tone of voice as you described your emotion. Listen for the music of your heart's song. Bear witness to yourself in the truth of your emotion. Your feelings are important, and you matter. That is success!

Waves of Living

Everything you do to *not feel* robs you of energy, leaving you shrunken, in a space too small for the miracle of who you are. How much space do you have for your richness and complexity? Each vulnerable point of contact, as your longing meets limits, stirs unrest and heralds a wave of emotion for you to ride to a new shore of yourself. Sometimes this will be quick and easy and smooth, a single low roller taking you there. Other times the waves will be high and choppy and demand your very best surfing skills. It takes courage to stay on the wave until it carries you to the shore, so be kind to yourself as you feel the flow and trust you will be taken to where you are more calm, clear, and connected to your deepest self.

Yours is not a flat-line life. Flux and flow are the way of things. Experience your emotions as they inform and energize your life. That is the reality and the gift of your human vulnerability: the brave, beautiful, heartbreaking, breathtaking, and glorious mission of growth.

8

unmasking your trickster defenses

"Love takes off masks that we fear we cannot live without and know we cannot live within."

JAMES BALDWIN

SERENA WAS a perfectionist. Which meant, of course, that nothing she did was good enough. In our first appointment she tore up and rewrote her check because her signature was not centered on the line. Bright, with interests ranging from economics to international culture, art, and design, Serena looked like Renée Zellweger from her Bridget Jones days. She did not date, she lived alone, and she had almost no friends but said that was fine with her. She dropped out of university after second year—every course graded either A-plus or Incomplete because she was so often paralyzed by procrastination.

Unable to bear making an error, Serena was working in a junior office job where she checked and rechecked her work and rewrote emails, worrying which font to use. Serena struggled to get out the door in the morning because she had to change her outfit several times, but she was never late because she set her watch twenty minutes fast. If someone remarked on her edgy European clothing sense, she heard criticism, so she would give off an icy air and withdraw. At the grocery checkout, she would have her debit card in hand before the clerk gave the total to avoid being humiliated by fumbling for it.

Serena was in hiding, covering her shame with perfectionistic behavior and pretending not to care. Her inner critic was running her life, raising the stakes perilously high so that dating, making friends, reaching for more challenging work, or trying anything new felt like existential threats. I invited her to let us know her more intimately and she grimaced. "It's better to be lonely than rejected," she said. She expected everyone, including me, to shun her. Hiding felt like a solution to Serena, a way to protect herself from the pain of rejection. Paying attention to her inner self felt intrusive and threatening. She couldn't see that although hiding felt like a solution, it was creating other problems.

Serena had been a sensitive, intense child whose young, overwhelmed mother locked herself in the bathroom when Serena had tantrums. Serena's much older father was easily frustrated and ill-equipped to help with her big feelings. When her distress escalated, he mocked or roared at her, sending her to her room. She cried herself to exhaustion, and when no one came to comfort her, she concluded she was unlovable, and her feelings were too much. "I hate the thought of needing anyone. I never want to depend on anyone again. I hate myself for letting my parents hurt me," she said.

"That makes sense to me," I said. "Who wouldn't want to hide from that kind of pain?" As she lifted her eyes toward me,

I said, "You are so brave to come here today, to reach out for help."

Serena looked away. "I don't want to see his look of disgust ever again," she declared. "Of course, you don't," I said. "No one wants to be looked at that way. Would it be okay to notice together what's happening in your body right now?" She growled, "You don't know how awful, how truly awful it is to be looked at like that!"

"Please tell me how awful," I said. "What's happening inside you right now as you remember that?" Serena was struggling to breathe, taking little sips of air and shielding her chest with crossed arms. "I'm choking and I'm just so angry! I hate feeling this way!" she fumed. "I should have bit my tongue. I should have been quiet. I should have been different. I brought it on myself."

Serena began to collapse under the weight of her self-attack. I asked her to stand back and pay attention inside. "Notice right here and now, it's just the two of us. Even though you're remembering being rejected, no one is rejecting you right now. Do you feel I'm judging you?" I asked. "No, I don't think so," she said. "Okay. Let's care about you right now. Let's stop judging you and ignoring you. Can you notice the tension inside you right now, in your arms and legs and chest?"

My invitation brought Serena into the present moment, and she took a deep breath. "It's so tense it hurts," she said. "Like I'm encased in something, and I can't move."

"Can you stay with it?" I asked. Serena nodded and after several moments of experiencing and describing the painful tension, she noticed a shift. "My shoulders have dropped, and my butt isn't as clenched. It's like something is melting." Serena was surprised to feel a small sense of relief in her body. "This is what happens when you're allowed to just be you and feel you," I said.

As we focused on her physical experience, she realized how she braced against imagined criticism all the time. "I *can't* just be me; I can't trust myself," she said. "My feelings are too big and I can't control them. If I let go, I'll blow apart." Serena felt her only option was to crush herself with criticism. "At least that way I won't be open and no one else can hurt me."

Serena was at the edge of a familiar black hole, the one she faced as a small child. "But this time you're not alone. You are with yourself," I said. "Let's look at what you're feeling in your body one more time."

Serena felt her tense, queasy stomach. "I'm sick of myself," she said. I asked her to simply observe that rejecting voice and focus warm attention on her body. She described the sensations slowly and precisely, and after a few moments her stomach began to feel better and the tension in her arms and butt eased. She looked at me shyly and shook her head. "I feel a softness around my heart. I don't usually feel anything inside except empty and sick."

As we sat with that experience, Serena seemed surprised that nothing "bad" was happening. Then she began to cry, softly at first, opening into quiet sobs. When her wave of grief passed, Serena's face was soft and open. She met my eyes for a moment, then her habitual shame took over. She blushed and said, "I had a meltdown."

"You melted for sure. Your warm attention melted the icy shell that's encased you for so long. Your shame melted," I said. She blinked her eyes wide. "Wow!" she said. "I've been frozen with shame my whole life."

Over the next months we listened to her body as she blocked the familiar critical voice, and Serena noticed she was becoming less perfectionistic. She began to try new things. She took a painting course and discovered she loved watercolors. She joined a gym, went on a solo vacation to Europe, and began to socialize with people from work. We explored her complex feelings toward her parents, whom she deeply loved. Though they had done their best and loved Serena, their shortcomings had also taught her it was better to hate herself than to feel the pain of her aching need for their love and comfort.

Serena prioritized paying attention to unrest and leaned in to feel her anger and grief and love. Over time she was asserting herself at work and with her family. "I don't let people walk on me anymore. And I don't have to act like I don't care."

Serena recalled how she'd learned to make her face expressionless so she wouldn't reveal her pain or longing, and she began to express herself more openly. "I want to know what I want and who I am, and I'm ready to let others know me, too," she said as she gestured with her hand over her heart. "I've been hidden from everyone, but mainly from myself. Now I know there's a spark inside me and I matter."

Serena, like many of us, had layers of defenses blocking access to emotion, creating suffering. She came in to see me driven by anxious stories and shame, pretending not to care. She grew her capacity to matter in her bodily experience. She learned how perfectionism covered her shame, and shame covered her anger and grief about her parents' inability to comfort her as a child. "I convinced myself I didn't care. But that lie was crushing me. I believed that if I were better or stronger, I wouldn't have needed love and comfort. And then they couldn't have hurt me. But I do care, and I want to care. The best feelings I've ever had were when I was hugged or comforted."

Serena saw her strength was not in crushing her longing for care, but in risking feeling it.

She came to see that denying the truth takes a lot of energy. She stopped ignoring herself in her body and claimed her right to matter. "I can tolerate the hurt now; it's better than the armor. Being able to love and be loved is the best thing about me. I've learned that I can be hurt and I'm still okay. I'm okay because I'm still with me."

Disconnecting from the Truth: Defenses

Anything you do to disconnect from the discomfort of unrest and emotion is a defense. Defenses are tricksters because they seem to make you feel better in the moment. You play sixteen quick games of online solitaire and distract from the anger you feel at your neighbor for not returning the pruning shears you loaned him. You escape from what does not *feel* good, and that seems to *be* good. But those disconnections from the truth, if enduring and habitual, block growth and lead to suffering.

We all use defenses at least some of the time. Defenses can be common behaviors, like joking or checking email or organizing a closet or exercising. Those ordinary behaviors become defenses when we use them with the underlying (often unconscious) purpose of removing ourselves from unrest and emotion.

Used flexibly, defenses get you through challenging situations until fully experiencing what you feel is safe. For example, if your supervisor is pontificating like the boss from *The Office*, you might imagine a trio of scary clowns breaking down his door and kidnapping him to distract yourself from the impulse to lunge at him with the stapler. Problem solved.

But habitually using defenses creates suffering. Defenses are the "pathology" in "psychopathology." You drink to not feel and become an alcoholic; you restrict food to not feel and become anorexic or compulsive; you obsess about things to not feel and become paralyzed with indecision; you work too much to not feel and lose balance, health, and your close relationships with others. Or, like Serena, you criticize yourself to not feel your longing for closeness and become encased in shame, isolated and alone.

When your defense is doing its job, you won't feel unrest. Unrest is an inner call heralding emotion. The purpose of your defense is to disconnect you from that. By the time your defense has kicked in, you have been kicked out! It's hard to recognize when you've left home because it just feels normal to be scrolling your Facebook feed or micromanaging your partner.

Flagging your habitual defenses alerts you to when you leave yourself. Then you can keep your eyes open for your favorite exits and block them, come home, and feel.

Attend or Defend

If you believe what is inside you is worthless, unlovable, or dangerous, then you love your defenses more than yourself. Mattering requires noticing and blocking defenses, soothing unrest, and feeling your emotional truth, even if it is scary and hard.

You *cannot* give up your defenses until you notice them. And you *will not* give up your defenses until you see their cost. But if you do not notice you are leaving, how can you assess the price and choose to come home?

The purpose of this chapter is to help you see *how* you disconnect, so you have the choice to come home. This is the back door to growth; the front door is catching unrest the moment it knocks. But if (like many of us) your defenses are so automatic that you "leave home" before you sense unrest, then you can look in the mirror and see what it reflects. Maybe you don't feel your unrest spiking with an urge to run or don't notice your feet hitting the deck, but when you look in the mirror, you can see you are on a treadmill, sweating up a storm, and getting nowhere.

Defenses are just that because of their *function*, which makes them tricky to identify. If you are doing, thinking, or feeling something to *avoid experiencing core emotion*, then you are defending. The very same behavior, thought, or feeling in another context is simply what it appears to be. For example, I can go for a long run to stay fit, or I can go for a long run to numb my anger about a conflict that I do not want to deal with. Only you know the truth of your motivations.

Defenses are also tricky because they feel natural, protective, even good for you. The clinical term is *ego-syntonic*. You don't see your defense; it just seems like who you are. A "compliant pleaser" who avoids conflict says, "I never get mad; I'm just an easygoing person." A person who picks fights says, "I'm just scrappy; I have to stand up for myself." But those folks don't see how they create situations they don't like, as when the compliant person never gets their way, or the scrappy person repeatedly loses friends and jobs.

Psychotherapists study long and hard to develop expertise in defense work. We identify defenses and gently make clients aware of their existence, roots, function, and costs. We help people see their defenses as learned habits that were once adaptive but now create suffering. Depending on how established our defensive structure has become, it can be necessary to work with a professional to identify and undo these overlearned patterns.

Still, many of us can become aware of and learn to block defenses. In the next section, I share a framework to help you recognize some ways you exit yourself, so you can choose to come home when unrest calls.

When Unrest Calls and You Leave Home

Defenses remove you from unrest and emotion by disconnecting you from yourself (*intrapsychic defenses*) or from others (*interpersonal defenses*). Intrapsychic defenses detach you internally from what you feel. Interpersonal defenses wall you off from or project movies onto others.

In our defensive patterns, we are like snowflakes; none of us is exactly alike. But so that you simply start to recognize some, we will look only at intrapsychic defenses. I have grouped them into four patterns of "relating with yourself": *neglectful, anxious, critical,* and *masking.* For each pattern I've created an exercise with three questions to help you identify if that is how you defend against your feelings. Carefully reflect on each question, looking within for sensations and thoughts that will help you know how you have left home. A fourth step gives you instruction on how to disentangle yourself from the tricky grip of your defense.

The Neglectful Relationship:
Minimizing and Distracting

When you brush off your inner experience as "no big deal," you are neglectful. You ignore or minimize what you feel. Indifference to discomfort seems like strength and caring about pain seems like weakness. You fear you'll lose your "edge" or lose control. You may believe paying attention to feelings is indulgent, or simply wasting time, because there's no *point* in feeling.

You can be neglectful by *thinking things* that discount what you feel. Examples of cognitive neglect include denial, humor, minimizing, suppressing, rationalizing, and intellectualizing. You can also be neglectful by *doing things* to escape from your feelings. Examples of behavioral neglect include shopping, helping others, eating, drinking, scrolling social media, exercising, working, housecleaning, and watching cute kitten videos.

PRACTICE: YOUR NEGLECT-IDENTIFICATION QUESTIONS

1 Do you feel irritated at the thought of tuning in to your inner experience?

2 When you tune in to your body, do you notice dismissive messages, like "don't be a whiner" or "what a waste of time" or "that tension is just from sitting at my desk too long today"?

3 If you resist the urge to ignore what you feel, does unrest increase? There's often a sense of urgency behind defenses, compelling us to engage in them. For example, if you resist purchasing something and notice yourself agitated, irritable, distracted, and obsessing, you may be using shopping as a defense to avoid feeling. If you don't play your computer game or don't have that glass of wine or don't eat the junk food, what happens inside? Similarly, if you don't let yourself ruminate on the possible reasons your friend was half an hour late, yet again, what arises inside you?

WHAT TO DO: Be aware of resistance to noticing neglect. Noticing neglect is the first step to correcting it. Be curious about how you detach from feelings and link that detachment to how stuck or empty you feel, so you can matter. If you notice unrest, that is success! Even though you feel more uncomfortable, you are successful because now you see *how* you have been avoiding what you feel. You can now block the defense, soothe your body, and feel what is true for you.

The Anxious Relationship:
Control and Hypervigilance

An anxious relationship toward your experience arises from the fantasy that you can have control and certainty. It leads to worry, indecision, panic episodes, and even hypochondriasis (the unwarranted fear of having an illness).

Rather than ignoring, you fearfully scan for and misinterpret bodily arousal, while also scanning the external world for potential danger. You operate on the principle, "Better safe than sorry." You believe if you focus fretfully about the future or ruefully about the past, you'll be safer than if you inhabit the moment and trust your capacity to cope.

Worry

Worry brings with it a (false) sense of control. Worriers are certain they should worry, even when the odds for their fearful forecast are so low that they would be the winner of a reverse-luck lottery if their prediction came true. When you worry, you get lost in a story. You don't see you are *having worry thoughts to avoid feeling unrest.* You are sure something "out there" needs your attention. Worry distracts you from the vulnerable truth that you don't have ultimate control and certainty.

Shane needed to be "ready." "I need to prepare for everything, just in case," he said. I asked him to tell me the worst of his imaginings. "I'm afraid of what I see when I close my eyes—I see things not working out, and not being able to handle it, not being able to cope."

I invited him, "Close your eyes and look inside... You've been closing your eyes and looking *outside*. What you fear isn't located out there. It's in the discomfort of your body. Let's just be with that."

"I have known
a great many troubles
in my life, most of
which never happened."

MARK TWAIN

Shane spent that session focusing on physical tension, despite his strong urge to worry. He was surprised to discover how agitated he was. He was tense and buzzing from head to toe, yet all he had been aware of was mental worry. As he stayed with his physical experience, his nervous system began to settle.

I assigned Shane homework: every time he noticed he was worrying he was to block the thoughts and focus on sensations. He did this for several weeks, until one day he came in and told me, "This feeling-my-body thing seemed really weird at first, but I think I'm getting it. I'm more able to stay in the moment and nothing bad is happening! It feels brave actually, to be with that discomfort. And I feel calmer. I'm more 'with' myself. It's a different kind of ready."

Worry is not the same as healthy planning. It's looping through scary possibilities, imagining that the "what-ifs" will prevent or manage them. After many months of work to help one woman face and feel unrest, she said to me, with tears of self-compassion, "You mean the 'bad thing' I've been avoiding all this time is a feeling in my body? Just these sensations? I thought it was danger; I thought it was *something*."

The terrible irony is that when you avoid unrest and believe you cannot tolerate what it would feel like to have bad things happen, you live in an imagined world where bad things are happening over and over.

Indecisiveness and Regret

Some people avoid making decisions because they dread making the "wrong" one. Terms like "FOMO," for "fear of missing out," and "FOBO," for "fear of a better offer," reflect how common it is for people to anticipate being unable to bear the inevitable mixture of good and bad that comes with every decision. The idea that there are decisions with no downsides, the fantasy that you can know an outcome before it occurs, and the intolerance of your limits to control all contribute to difficulty with decisions.

Paralyzed with indecision, Charlene came to see me. She could not make up her mind about all sorts of things: what sofa to buy, which volunteer job to commit to, even choosing what day to make our appointment created stress for her. As we dug in deeper, Charlene saw that she did know what she wanted. "But," she said, "I still don't know what to *decide*, because what if it turns out later that I'm wrong? I don't want regret."

Charlene second-guessed and delayed decisions to avoid feeling vulnerable. But the price for that avoidance was paralysis. She couldn't move forward with career plans or relationship decisions or even purging old clothes she hadn't worn in years. Her expectation of perfect foresight and control made her a cruel judge of herself. She looked back with the benefit of hindsight and felt it was patently clear what she should have chosen.

As we looked at past decisions, I invited Charlene to see her vulnerability in the moment of deciding. Her need for certainty was so strong that she presented each outcome as perfectly foreseeable. If her decision had turned out well, she shrugged it off as obvious; if it had not, she ruminated over it and condemned herself. The breakthrough came when I asked her to tell me the worst decision she had made. Charlene slumped in her seat, her eyes filled with pain, and said, "I waited too long to fly home when my mother was dying."

"Tell me," I encouraged her. She shuddered and her hands came to her face. "I kept second-guessing myself. There were good reasons to go right away and good reasons to wait, and I couldn't decide. And then it was too late."

"Feel that, right now, in your body," I urged. Charlene nodded. She slowed down and described her muscles constricting and bracing. She went deeper, focusing on the shakiness, agitation, and tightness, with each breath connecting to her lost, rejected younger self. She shook her head and looked like she wanted to escape the session, escape her unrest, but instead she leaned in until her discomfort began to wane. And then she simply cried. All the tears that had frozen into paralysis and doubt melted. "I couldn't do it. I couldn't decide and I made a mistake and she died and I wasn't there. I will regret that for the rest of my life. I haven't even been able to think about my mother without feeling sick inside."

"This is punishment, not regret, Charlene," I said gently. "You need to feel your sadness instead of this awful, endless prison sentence. Instead of feeling sadness about your human limits and your loss, you're punishing yourself. Would your mother have wished that for you?" Charlene looked shocked at the thought. She sat up straight and said, "Absolutely not. My mother was kind and supportive."

"What might she say to you today then?" I asked. Charlene reflected awhile. "I think she would say that if it had been obvious that I needed to go right away, I would have gone! I did the best I could. I think she would forgive me." A weight lifted off her, and she looked upward. "I really didn't know what would happen, and I thought I had more time. I was wrong, but I was not bad. And I have paid the price a thousand times over. Maybe it's time to forgive myself."

Charlene confronted the terrible price for her defensive indecision. She felt sorrow for having missed her mother's passing. And she felt the love for her mother and for herself that had been blocked by regret. Charlene opened to accept herself as a vulnerable human. "I don't need certainty. I need compassion for myself. There is no crystal ball." Through facing uncertainty and soothing unrest, Charlene was moved by emotion to let go of paralyzing indecisiveness and regret.

Catastrophic Misinterpretation of Sensations

Catastrophic misinterpretation of physical sensations drives panic disorder and hypochondriasis. These folks watch for anxious feelings but, instead of soothing them, tell a frightening story. When I invite them to feel the body they tell me, "Oh for goodness' sake, Sandra! I feel my anxiety all the time! If that helped, I wouldn't be in this terrible state."

When you use bodily sensations as evidence of danger, you avoid rather than soothe them. People with panic disorder tell stories about humiliation, loss of control, and even death. People with hypochondriasis see the trembling as a symptom of Parkinson's disease, the dizziness as Ménière's disease, or the queasiness as likely stomach cancer.

Noticing bodily sensations and creating catastrophic stories about them is different from noticing and soothing them. And the difference is life altering.

PRACTICE: YOUR ANXIETY-IDENTIFICATION QUESTIONS

1 What is *actually* happening in this moment? Only danger warrants protective fight-or-flight action. Is it danger (in-the-moment threat to life and limb)? If yes, fight or flee. Is it vulnerability (emotion rising, uncertainty, limits to control—in other words, unrest)? If yes, soothe the body with warm interest and nonjudgment. Is it anxiety (threatening movies and stories about the future or past)? If yes, block the scary story and soothe the body. Note: "Future danger" is not danger; it is anxiety because it is not in the moment.

2 Does paying attention to sensations bring arousal down or keep it elevated? If the arousal does not come down, look for a movie or story running in the background preventing you from being present. The biggest clue that a scary movie is playing is

unyielding bodily arousal despite your patient, warm interest and nonjudgment.

3 Are you narrating what you are feeling, or are you in the moment, feeling your body?

WHAT TO DO: Remember that anxiety is the *exit* from unrest, generated by stories. Simply paying attention to bodily sensations while stories continue to run will not soothe your distress. You must distinguish anxiety from unrest. Unrest is soothed with attention, anxiety keeps returning. Name the story and see how it tries to take you away from vulnerable reality. Decide not to give that story any more of your energy. Then feel unrest until it melts in the warmth of your inner attention.

The Critical Relationship: Self-Attack

If you blame and shame yourself, you are in a critical relationship with your inner life. Self-attack is so consuming it distracts you from the painful truth of your limits.

Self-attack is a way some people punish themselves for feeling anger toward those they love. If self-criticism is a deep-seated habit, you may have learned in childhood that anger leads to abandonment and adapted by attacking and abandoning yourself when anger threatens to rise. You criticize yourself, saying if you tried harder or were smarter, or were a better person or more lovable or more attractive or stronger or not as gullible or more patient or acted sooner or, or, or… then things would go better. When something doesn't work out, you may even blame yourself for wanting it. Rather than feel loss and grow, you turn against your longing, as though if you don't have complete control, you shouldn't even want things.

The antidote is to see these attacks as lies and block them. Blocking inner putdowns does not mean ignoring them; ignoring empowers them. Blocking does not mean debating or fighting with them. Those old stories have been running a long time. Your little cognitive arguments will be ineffective against the emotional heft of these aggressions.

To block self-attack you need to see the *function* of the criticism: to deny the reality of your limits. You need to see the *price* of rejecting yourself: flattened emotional experience, eventually creating depression. When you see self-criticism as a trick in your head to get you out of your body, you can detach from it and direct your full attention to soothing unrest.

PRACTICE: YOUR SELF-ATTACK IDENTIFICATION QUESTIONS

1 Do I suffer from depression? Self-attack is almost always at the heart of depression.

2 Do I feel more energized or drained after listening to those messages? (These criticisms do not motivate you in a positive way.)

3 Is it possible I learned to turn against myself rather than feel angry with my parents or others?

WHAT TO DO: Your inner litany of self-criticism can be so familiar that you may not notice the insults, so cataloging the usual suspects is useful. When you recognize the critical voice saying, "stupid" or "worthless" or "not good enough," wake up. Feel offended. The faster you do, the faster you can say, "I know where you want to take me, and I'm not going along." You are declaring that you would rather feel vulnerable than hated.

The Emotional Masquerade

If it looks like sadness and walks like sadness and talks like sadness, is it sadness? Aren't all emotions just what they appear to be?

Nope. Sometimes *other feelings* are employed as defenses.

Defensive emotion is learned. In early life, certain feelings were more acceptable than others and safer to reveal. Defensive emotions operate (at a subconscious level) to keep you away from vulnerable core emotion. Feelings as defenses can be difficult to perceive in yourself because they *feel* real. However, there are three clues to identifying defensive emotions.

The first clue is that defensive emotions do not stir unrest. They create a cover story that's less threatening than your real emotion. Defenses remove you from the vulnerability of what you truly feel. There's no vulnerability in a feeling that's not a true emotion, so there's no unrest. For example, if you got angry when you were little and your parents shamed you, you may have learned to act helpless and sad instead. Perhaps that earned a kind response, or at least you avoided rejection. So now, when you're angry, rather than straightening your spine and speaking up for yourself, you collapse into weepy tears and act small. You do not do this consciously; it's an automatic reflex, and you probably think you are sad. But your faux-sad reaction does not evoke unrest. When you are using a faux feeling to cover the true one (like weepiness to cover healthy anger) the weepiness solves the vulnerability problem. You are not vulnerable because the truth of your anger is hidden. If you block the defensive weepiness, your unrest will rise because your anger will start to emerge, as you connect with what is true.

A second clue to identify defensive emotion is that it feels like a steady state; it doesn't move in a wavelike fashion, rising, cresting, and ebbing. A defensive feeling kind of rises and then flatlines. The anger just goes on and on without relief, or the sadness seems without end. Core emotion always rises and falls and brings relief at the end.

Third, defensive emotion does not take you to a new place of understanding or connection when you feel it. You loop and loop, telling yourself the same litany of stories and feeling a frustrated sense of going nowhere.

Here are three examples of defensive emotions: anger to cover sadness, sadness to cover anger, and guilt to cover anger. But since any feeling can be used to cover another, there are many more tricksters, such as manic energy to cover sadness, shame to cover anger, anger to cover healthy guilt, or sexual feelings to cover anger.

Anger to Cover Sadness

Brian came to my office talking about his father, who used to beat him up as a kid. He was agitated and annoyed as he spoke. He was dismissive with me when I asked him to give me the details and fidgety and irritable as I asked him to focus on the sensations in his body. Then he got mad at himself because he couldn't seem to "do it right." Session after session, the same pattern emerged, regardless of the topic. Was he an angry man? In fact, yes, but not yet.

Despite his presentation, what Brian was, mostly, was sad. He had tears he could not cry about wrongs that could not matter. He shoved all his grief into a capsule encased in titanium. The pressure in his heart was intense. It felt explosive. It scratched at him. As frustrating as that daily battle was, his anger felt preferable, in some ancient part of him, to facing the deep well of sorrow at not having mattered enough to be kept safe as a child.

Precise defense work and embodied exploration brought Brian to the place where he could feel the grief of his tragic lack of safety. The dam burst and he wept for himself and for the little boy he once was, who had only wanted to be loved. The terrible violation, once grieved, could then be protested.

We looked at his father's rage and Brian felt his own reactive, protective anger. He saw that expressing anger in childhood would have evoked a dangerous escalation of his father's attacks. He'd needed to cover over his natural reaction. Brian felt the hot energy of his anger helping him stand up for himself, until he finally felt he mattered. He felt how he'd wanted to be safe and loved and deserved that. Having faced the complex mixture of his feelings, Brian was no longer impatient and irritable. He was free to feel, comfortable in his skin.

Sadness to Cover Anger

Debbie came to me with complaints of being taken advantage of. She said she did everything "right" and yet never got what she wanted. Her efforts to get an education and a career were obstructed by her parents and later by her husband. Now, she was divorced and lonely; she felt misunderstood and inhibited in her ambitions.

As she told me all this, her eyes welled up with tears and she crumpled over. Was she sad? No and yes. Mainly she was angry, but she didn't dare know that.

As an attuned child, Debbie was easy to shape with shame. Her mother was a long-suffering martyr and expected Debbie to go along with the program. Debbie's best chance at praise was to put her feelings aside and wait patiently to be seen. Her tears were not soothed but at least elicited some attention. Her anger was met with cold rejection. Debbie developed a defensive pattern of sadness to cover anger.

Debbie's first attempts to look at examples of being thwarted stirred weepiness and feelings of impotence. We zeroed in on a specific situation at work where she sacrificed herself for a particularly demanding and unappreciative boss. As we dug underneath her teary powerlessness, Debbie saw that she was angry at being treated so dismissively. But as soon as the anger arose, tears leaked from her eyes. I asked her, "What might happen if you don't wash your anger away with tears? Would you like to feel more powerful?"

Debbie sat up straight and leaned forward with a clear, "Yes!" It took many tries but eventually she could regulate unrest and let anger strengthen her. We worked with this energy until Debbie understood how being denied her right to protest as a child had disabled her adult assertion. She came to see how her learned habit contributed to her suffering.

When Debbie felt safe enough to understand the price she had paid for her martyrdom, boy, was she angry! She was also delighted. It felt true and powerful to connect with her assertion. We worked through many waves of healthy anger until she felt entitled to speak up and stand up for herself, and reach for what she wanted. After she metabolized her anger, Debbie processed deep and genuine sadness, freeing herself to live with more purpose and power.

Guilt to Cover Anger

Yvonne came in feeling bad about herself and told me her widowed mother repeatedly criticized her for not spending enough time with her. Yvonne had been giving her mother as much time and attention as she could. But no matter how often Yvonne visited or how much she helped out, her mother let her know Yvonne was a disappointment.

When I asked what her feeling was toward her mother, she said she felt guilty, because her mother was alone and needed help and didn't have many friends. But was she actually guilty? No and yes.

Guilt is a healthy feeling when we have wronged another person. But had Yvonne done or said anything "wrong"? Had she been rude or abusive or disrespectful? No, she had not. She had not done what her mother wanted. Yvonne could not be feeling real guilt toward her mother, since she hadn't done anything wrong.

Her mother's disappointment reflected her mother's expectations, not Yvonne's actions. Failing to live up to another person's expectations is not a violation against them. Putting expectations on others is a violation, and the healthy feeling about that violation is anger. Yvonne was angry about being regarded as a constant disappointment, but she covered her anger with guilt so she didn't have to face the pain of her anger toward someone she loved.

Her anger, when she eventually let herself feel it, allowed her to set better boundaries. Yvonne accepted her mother as a separate person with a right to her feelings and saw her mother's disappointment as a reflection of her mother's expectations, not of Yvonne's shortcomings. Yvonne's anger released her from toxic guilt and reconnected with her loving feelings toward her mother, and self-respecting feelings toward herself.

PRACTICE: YOUR MASQUERADE-IDENTIFICATION QUESTIONS

1 Do you feel unrest when you feel a particular feeling? Real emotion comes with unrest, signaling the vulnerability of being moved by something true. Defensive feeling doesn't evoke unrest because it is a defense, covering the feeling underneath that is vulnerable and true.

2 Does the feeling crest and ebb like a wave, or does it plateau, leaving you stuck?

3 Do you find yourself in a new place at the end of the feeling? Do you feel clearer, with more understanding or energy or connection?

WHAT TO DO: When you notice yourself cycling in a feeling that doesn't seem to vary in intensity and doesn't take you anywhere, consider the possibility that it is a trick to cover your real feeling. Ask yourself, "If I didn't feel this right now, what *else* might I feel?"

The Sense in Defense
(A Tuna Sandwich Past Its Shelf Life)

Once you see your defenses, you may be tempted to judge yourself for what seem to be senseless or destructive patterns. Those behaviors can make you feel impatient toward yourself. But your defensive reaction is part of the human reflex to avoid discomfort and pain, and perhaps helped you cope at another time and place. You must approach your defenses with curiosity and compassion.

Remember that tuna sandwich you made? You know the one. You made it and took it to work to eat at lunchtime. It was nutritious and delicious, with protein and carbs and energy for your day. But that was a very hectic day and, busy and distracted, you didn't get to it. It was shoved in the back of a desk drawer and forgotten. Days passed, until an unpleasant odor emanated from your desk, and you opened the drawer and found the wax-paper-covered slimy mess that was once your sandwich. That unrecognizable thing that was once something you would have eaten, that would have been good for you, was now toxic. It was past its shelf life.

So it is with defensive reactions. Underneath today's habitual defenses lies something else: a healthy need or feeling that seems not safe enough to reveal. For example, Zach had an interpersonal defense of suspecting the worst motives in others. His air of hostility evoked negative reactions from people. In our work together, he was moved to uncover his deep desire to trust. That healthy longing was hidden because his childhood environment was so unsafe. His defensive mistrust, stinky and unhealthy as a rotten tuna sandwich, was originally an attempt to get something life affirming: safety. By not trusting others and even suspecting the worst of them, he could avoid the pain of being betrayed and imagine he was safe. But his longing to trust was healthy and nutritious, and something he needed. When he saw the purpose of his defense, he could block it, experience closeness, and learn new, more mature ways to protect himself.

Faith

Resistance to feeling is normal. Defenses come with being human. You need faith to lean toward discomfort, uncertain if you can bear it and not knowing what you will find beneath. You risk feeling pain if things are not the way you wish. As you put down your defensive swords and shields, you open to heartache. That seems like a bad idea.

Growth asks you have faith in a force that wants you to be whole. That force is emotion, wired into your body, at a cellular level. Faith in your body's intelligence, in its ability to heal and grow with the flow of emotion, helps you block defenses that say what you are experiencing is unimportant or dangerous or a sign of weakness. With that faith, you can answer the body's call as it invites you into the present moment.

Unless you are in physical danger, your body wants to release tension. It wants to be soft, open, and receptive. It wants to feel your attention, to feel cared for, to feel the truth. Your body does not want to be whipped or neglected or bracing. You don't mature by armoring against life. A tulip does not grow because it is shielded. It grows because it receives what it needs to grow. You are meant to receive emotional experiences.

The feelings rising up just want to be accompanied, and when you regulate unrest, they will carry you to a good place. You don't yet know what that place looks like, but if you go with the flow, you'll get to know.

You want to understand first, then (perhaps) to feel. Instead, say to yourself, "Let's experience this first, *then* understand." Notice unrest and open to the moment. Discomfort is part of the process. Faith helps you say, "This is hard, but it's okay."

Think of a child learning to ride a bike. She needs to develop balance. But she can't achieve that through cognitive understanding. The concept of balance will not help her. Only the experience of balance will do that. She just needs to do it. She has to let go and feel gravity and momentum in her body. She needs to wobble and correct and maybe crash a few times before she gets it. Experiencing all this grows her balance until she discovers that she can ride like the wind.

As you step forward in faith you make little moment-to-moment choices that bring you toward your experience of emotion. Like that little girl learning to ride, you make small corrections as you move forward into the wind. You can slow down. You can breathe. You can notice you are caught up in a defense. You can turn away from the defense and embrace discomfort, noticing the shift in your muscle tension. You can decide you're worth taking a chance on.

Bring attention to your exhaled breath as you surrender to what is, in this moment, in the body. Stop arguing about what should be and be with what is. Then you experience a different way of knowing, a bodily knowing. You may think nothing is happening because the chatter stops. It is quiet inside, organic, like water sinking into sand. Now what is inside you is not alone and as a result is changed, opened up, moving from fear to love.

Consistency, Not Constancy

You do not need, on this journey of growth, to do it right all the time. What you need is consistency, not constancy. Commit to being present more often than not as you cycle through the steps of this process. Come back to your body just one more time than you leave, so it comes to trust your warm attention. Even if you've spent years ignoring unrest, avoiding answering your call to growth and sending all your body's messages to voicemail, it is never too late. You can take the call now.

The capacity to direct your attention is a superpower you can develop and strengthen. It lets you focus on what you choose, even when habitual forces whisper that "bodily discomfort is danger," "feeling is weakness," and "you are not and should not be vulnerable."

You can return to what matters over and over: the unrest in your body and the truth in your heart.

9

engaging the world with intimacy, influence, and inspiration

"What is fundamentally beautiful is compassion for yourself and those around you. That kind of beauty inflames the heart and enchants the soul."

LUPITA NYONG'O

YOUR JOY, aliveness, and ease are far and away enough reason to approach what doesn't feel good in your body and ride waves of emotion to more you. But when you soothe unrest, your calm nervous system can also relax the nervous systems of those around you. You show up in the world in an openhearted way that fosters intimacy with others, you influence them to contribute their gifts, and inspire them to reach for their dreams and serve the world.

Do you want to create safety and closeness with people you care about? Would you like to have greater influence in your working life? Do you dream of nudging society toward more justice and compassion? You can think of sharing your new way of being in three spheres: close relationships, work, and society. You deepen *intimacy* in your personal life, expand your *influence* at work, and become an *inspiration* for change in the larger world.

Intimacy

Being happy means being close with others. Measures of mental health, physical health, longevity, and productivity all underscore how your connection with others underpins every aspect of well-being.

When you bring your capacity to embrace unrest and feel emotion to being a parent or a partner or a friend, you create safety. You can listen with an open heart and express yourself honestly. In accepting your own vulnerability, you create space for others to accept theirs. In being strong enough to be moved, you can amplify others' joy, soothe their distress, and ease their pain. Your relationships begin to shimmer with aliveness and immediacy.

Cheryl came to see me for help with the anxiety of her eight-year-old daughter, Dawn. Cheryl and her family had just moved, and the circumstances were not happy. They'd moved in with her husband's parents after he lost his job during the COVID-19 pandemic. Dawn was complaining of tummy aches, worrying, having trouble sleeping. She was struggling to adjust to her new school and home routines. Cheryl was sad and stressed but doing her best to put on a brave, happy face.

Although helping Dawn with her anxiety was our primary goal, our first task involved Cheryl facing the truth of her own feelings. Since she and her husband had good reasons to move, Cheryl felt she needed to toughen up and ignore what she felt. "There's no point in focusing on that," she said, when I invited her to explore how recent changes had disrupted her life. "It's no big deal." But as she observed her braced body and held breath Cheryl saw that, although she wished it didn't matter, her body was saying otherwise.

I invited her to notice and soothe unrest so she could face the pain of "having to leave the neighborhood of my dreams, where I had friends and a garden and privacy." The daily challenges of living with her in-laws, loss of privacy and independence, and uncertainty of how or when they could get back on their feet all stirred an urge to brace against herself. Cheryl practiced noticing unrest until she could reliably identify it in her raised shoulders, tight glutes, and held breath. Those sensations became Cheryl's cue to slow down and tune in to her body, and over time she grew confident in her ability to come home.

Now Cheryl could face how angry she was at not having control over her husband's job situation and its impact on her life, and how sad she was about all she'd had to give up. Her hot wave of anger carried her into painful tears of grief, as Cheryl opened to accepting her limits. As she allowed herself to feel, Cheryl was surprised that she became calmer and more grounded. She felt like she mattered. She felt stronger and realized she was thankful for the kindness of her in-laws. Rather than continuing to shame herself into counting her blessings, Cheryl accessed genuine feelings of gratitude. She also realized her most important job was to show up with more capacity to bear her daughter's disappointment and ease her transition.

Cheryl had been avoiding her own feelings and unconsciously making her daughter feel unsafe to have hers. Dawn (as children do) had unerringly pinpointed her mother's emotional block. Cheryl came to see that as her unrest rose, her tolerance for her daughter's distress fell. Dawn's upset feelings triggered upset feelings in her mother, and since Cheryl was not allowed to feel, her daughter needed to settle down and cheer up, too. Cheryl's relentless optimism left Dawn alone in the constraint of "look on the bright side" and gave her no way to soothe her unrest. That made her anxiety rise as she began to worry about doing well at her new school and fitting in with other kids.

Cheryl's ability to soothe unrest allowed her to calmly lead the way for Dawn to talk about what was hard. As her daughter described how sad she was at leaving her friends and her favorite teachers, Cheryl was stirred; her own sadness began to resonate. But instead of ignoring unrest and automatically shutting herself and Dawn down, Cheryl slowed and tuned in to her body with warm interest.

With tears rimming her eyes and her body calm, Cheryl showed Dawn her feelings were important and real and not too much for her mother. Dawn opened up and poured out her heart to her mother and, for the first time in a long time, she felt safe. Dawn's anxiety was tamed; she could face her feelings and adjust to her new life with more ease. And Cheryl forged a safer and more intimate bond with her daughter.

How do you connect intimately with family, friends, and life partners? Through feeling and sharing vulnerable emotion. But when is it hardest to connect with others? When you are feeling vulnerable emotion. Now, instead of you both bracing and resisting being moved by each other's feelings, you can lead the way and bring others with you into a more regulated state where feelings are safe. Your regulated body is like the steady rhythm of a metronome that helps others find and keep the beat of the shared music of emotion. You feel together.

PRACTICE: REV UP AND RAMP DOWN

The emotion and distress of others, especially those you love, resonates in *your* body, and vice versa. So, the first job in fostering closeness with others is to soothe yourself, and *then* tune in to the other. The best way to get better at doing that is to think of examples of being activated and practice soothing them in your imagination.

Picture an emotion-laden interaction with a close person in your life. Perhaps your younger brother calls you to talk about his divorce, or your father is worried about his heart palpitations, or your neighbor tells you she has an infestation of carpet beetles, or your dear friend tells you she must euthanize her dog, or your partner tells you they're upset you forgot to pick up the groceries on your way home.

Vividly imagine the interaction and notice what happens in your body. Feel yourself rev up. Stay with those sensations with warm interest and nonjudgment until you feel your arousal come down. Good job! Now do it again. And again. And again. Keep doing it until the arousal feels almost friendly, like a signal to pay attention but nothing more.

Now your body knows its activation does not signal danger, so you're free to attune to another person's experience. Feel the vibration of their emotion as it resonates in your body, as you are moved. That will feel like a lot, because now it is two people sharing in the vulnerable truth of emotion. But you can do this. You soothe unrest, over and over, as you create a larger inner world for connecting with others. You share in the richness of two hearts and two minds dancing together. You model for others the courage to accept discomfort and create opportunities for those you care about to experience the safety and intimacy that emerge from engaging vulnerably.

Influence

One factor that makes work "work" is the need to manage your emotions to suit the requirements of the job. When you're skilled at soothing unrest, you can engage confidently during moments of uncertainty, when feelings run high. When you know how to feel safe in your body, you can create safety for others in your workplace. Your ability to deal well with frustration, delays, the unexpected, and other people's reactivity makes you someone others look to and look up to. You have *influence*. Colleagues, clients, patients, students, customers, and other contacts feel your presence and are more willing to share with you and listen to you.

Let's look at how the capacity to regulate unrest and access emotion fosters influence in the workplace, using examples from education, health care, and business.

Teachers

Cora told me how, as a grade-four student, she was so traumatized by her mother's violent rages and narcissistic emotional drama that she almost turned to granite to survive. In class each day she would sit, stone-faced, unable to engage with the other children, never raising her hand to answer a question, feeling trapped. Somehow her teacher sensed Cora's inner prison. Every day she smiled warmly and spoke softly to Cora with a word or two of encouragement, with no pressure to perform or take part, simply letting her know she was seen.

Cora looked forward to those moments of contact with her heart bursting. When her teacher smiled at her, she felt her frozen-self melt. Even though Cora never showed her teacher what that warm interest meant, as she shared this story decades later with tears of gratitude, she told me her teacher's attunement had saved her life. Her teacher had

"From joy I came,
for joy I live,
in sacred joy I melt."

PARAMAHANSA YOGANANDA

tuned in to her own body to perceive from Cora signals so subtle they would be imperceptible to others. And this gifted teacher's embodied response to gently lean toward Cora in her well-regulated way, with no need for Cora to do anything differently, seeded a feeling of self-worth that, many years later, bore fruit.

Education is more than teaching children information. It's also developing their capacities, especially for emotional regulation. Teachers are the vehicle through which these competencies are transmitted, but we've been asking them to grow children's abilities without first investing in the teachers themselves. These capacities are experiential and embodied and must be grounded in the teacher's ability to notice and soothe her own bodily signals.

To learn, children need to be within an optimal window of arousal: stimulated enough to pay attention (unlike Charlie Brown's teacher *wah wahing* until her students keel over snoring), but also calm enough to concentrate. These are physical experiences. A teacher's unregulated unrest sends unconscious signals to students that disrupt their sense of safety. How can teachers convey to children that they need to settle down if they are an unconsciously vibrating mix of unrest and anger? Teachers who are connected to their inner experience use their own bodies as a tuning fork. Their capacity to transmit joy and excitement and their capacity to calm themselves down form a foundation for entraining students' physiology.

Jeannette is an energetic French-immersion primary school teacher who came to see me to resolve issues arising out of the end of her marriage. After many months of that work, she arrived at her appointment and delightedly shared her plans to implement the practice of soothing unrest into her classroom. She told me how before each class she took a moment to connect into her body with warm interest to feel her unrest. Once she registered an inner shift, she warmly greeted each child as they entered the classroom, nodding and making sparkly eye contact with each one.

She began the class by inviting her students to look inside for today's *papillons* (butterflies) and then tame them with warm interest and slow breaths. In another exercise, called *"Dis bonjour avec les yeux"* (say hello with your eyes), the children were asked to greet each of the other students solely by making eye contact. Then they were asked to notice how their butterflies felt and tame them again.

Jeannette also role-modeled how emotion activates the body. For example, when the children were doing a good job of politely passing their papers to each other, she told them she was happy, and pointed to her lips and eyes curving up at the corners and her open, upright body posture. At moments when they were not listening, she asked the students to notice that Madame Jeannette was getting angry, "See how my jaw is tight, my legs are strong, and I'm planting my hands on my hips?" The kids soaked all this up naturally, like they were meant to learn their feelings in their bodies. She told me of one frustrated little boy having trouble learning who told her his arms and legs were telling him he was angry, and he needed to ask for help!

This committed, inspired teacher practiced what she learned with me, then taught it. Her students learned to notice their unrest, take care of it, identify emotion, and use it to resolve problems. Those primary-school children developed emotional competence to rival any forty-year-old!

Medical and Health-Care Professionals

We all saw dire images of overcrowded ICUs, makeshift tent hospitals, and exhausted, weeping doctors slumped in hallways during the COVID-19 pandemic. Up against impossible levels of demand and insufficient resources, physicians, nurses, and emergency personnel were sometimes forced to decide who received treatment and who did not, who lived and who died. Faced with these unimaginable choices and conditions, many could not take care of themselves and were sucked into a pit of over-functioning, overwhelm, despair, suicidal feelings, and burnout.

The pandemic was an event of global peril unprecedented in our lifetime. But health-care providers are confronted with human vulnerability every day. They face their own limits over patients' outcomes, exacerbated by feelings of responsibility toward people who come to them expecting help. Health-care workers treat patients who are in pain and afraid, unsure about their condition, and without much power in the system. Patients' distress can be deeply wearing, their bodies communicating unrest in their fidgety hands, braced muscles, shallow breathing. Health professionals may unwittingly shut down to block out discomfort that they do not realize they have. They may become impatient or judgmental or detached, giving health-related results, prognoses, or other information as though it has no emotional meaning. Yet it is essential to stay openhearted with patients to foster their feeling of being cared about, to inspire hope, and to motivate healthy behavior.

To care with compassion, the provider must be able to recognize and accept his own vulnerable limits. When he can soothe unrest and feel grief at his limits and face his pain at not being able to do what he would want, he can care more deeply about the patient's feelings while holding on to healthy boundaries. When a patient is accompanied with compassion in the uncertainty and emotional pain of illness, she is influenced to find the courage to face what must be faced.

François, who had been working with me for quite some time, came in one day with an eyepatch and told me he was awaiting an investigative procedure to determine if he might lose sight in his left eye. An avid skier, cyclist, hiker, and musician, he was facing awful uncertainty and limits to control, and we made space for his experience of vulnerability. We slowed as he tuned in to the spike of unrest in his body, and he let himself feel the agitation and tension until it waned. Sadness rose and he quietly shook his head and breathed heavily. As his body settled, he shared with me a remarkable experience he had shared with the ophthalmologist who'd given him the news. Somehow, in the way the doctor had been present with him, François had felt assured.

"The doctor wasn't guarding himself against anything," he said. "I could feel him being open to everything I was feeling. He was contained and caring but at the same time he gave me the message that if the worst happens, I'll be okay. It was less the words he used and more the way he was with me: the eye contact and lack of clamping down in his body, the confidence in his voice. I could feel he knows the reality of the risk and he's not denying it, but somehow, he believes in me, that no matter what the news, I can cope. I feel not alone. And I feel like I can do this." That is powerful influence.

Sadly, some research suggests medical training reduces students' empathy, particularly in third year. That is when students are first exposed to patients, usually with little guidance on the emotional realities of what it feels like to sit across from someone who is receiving a cancer diagnosis, being prepared for a risky medical procedure, being told they may never be able to walk again, and the like. With little understanding of the inevitable stirring of unrest as they come face to face with their patients' vulnerability and their own limits to control, many young interns ignore the troubling feelings inside them and shut down their hearts to get the job done. Unfortunately for their patients and themselves, a well-regulated nervous system and an empathic, open heart is what brings enhanced health results for the patient and, in the long run, meaning and satisfaction for the doctor.

The "active ingredient" in the provider-patient relationship is the provider's ability to soothe unrest and stay open to the patient. Whether in nursing, psychotherapy, physiotherapy, or any other health-care profession, when you understand patients *will* affect you and unrest *will* be stirred, you can soothe your physiology and use your calmed nervous system to coregulate, connect with, and motivate your patients.

Leaders in Business

True leadership is not the same as authority or power. It is social influence that draws forth peoples' best efforts and motivates them to achieve a goal. But people do not contribute in this way because you command them, or because of your title, or because you say you know best. In the words of Theodore Roosevelt, "Nobody cares how much you know until they know how much you care." Leaders evoke feelings in the people they want to influence, feelings that prompt them to step up and contribute their gifts to bring a vision alive. Conveying empathy, transmitting a vision, listening deeply, giving and receiving feedback, and being accountable and authentic are key qualities of a leader. Your capacity to soothe unrest is the invisible skill that underpins all those properties of leadership.

Uncertainty and limits to control are facts of life in every facet of human endeavor, including in the workplace. Recognizing moments of uncertainty and knowing how to tune in and regulate your nervous system allow you to lead with authenticity. Your well-regulated nervous system enhances your ability to access the emotional wisdom that inspires loyalty, dissolves conflict, empowers risk-taking, and fosters belonging.

People are motivated to give their best when they feel safe and seen. Your willingness to model being vulnerable, accepting and managing uncertainty rather than denying or shaming it, creates a culture where people will risk going beyond the familiar and give more than they must. Brené Brown's massively powerful work on leadership stresses the ability to embrace vulnerability: "If you're not willing to build a vulnerable culture, you can't create." But that embrace of vulnerability is not a cognitive process; it isn't something you simply decide to do. Leading vulnerably hinges upon your capacity to notice and soothe the physical feelings of unrest. That foundation allows you to read and respond to physical, nonverbal cues in yourself and others in a way that makes people feel like they matter. Your embodied inner connection reveals you as authentic and is a beacon for others, increasing their willingness to give their best and take risks in the safety that your comfort with vulnerability creates.

One of my leadership guides is Armand Gamache, the fictional police inspector created by author Louise Penny. He makes his junior officers adopt four phrases that reflect vulnerability and lead to wisdom: "I don't know," "I need help," "I am sorry," and "I was wrong." These statements demonstrate a particular kind of courage. Though he is our hero in the story, Monsieur Gamache is depicted as a vulnerable person affected by uncertainty and loss and limits to control. We watch as he is moved, sometimes torn, in situations of stress, by an inner emotional truth. We see him brace and then, taking a moment to settle his nervous system, exhale, as he gathers himself internally before orienting outward to lead others. The officers who follow his lead learn more about policing from these lessons in humanity than from any of their more traditional training and are galvanized to contribute their finest efforts and risk their lives.

But leadership is not just for corporate or military bosses. Bus drivers, checkout clerks, waiters—every one of us has a leadership role to play in the workplace. Having a well-regulated inner state and knowing how to pay attention in vulnerable moments will improve job performance, satisfaction, and success, and will also positively influence others. For example, a mechanic who knows how to regulate his unrest can prevent misunderstanding by listening carefully and communicating calmly, can address my frustration at a delay in fixing my car without being defensive, and is not oversensitive if I ask about the bill. As a result, I'm less likely to conflict with him, more likely to return to him for another repair, and more likely to refer my friends to him. I'm also more likely to tell him how much I appreciate his professionalism and service, making him feel valued and increasing his satisfaction and reward in his work.

A well-regulated presence matters in every walk of life. Several years ago, Karim got a job as an attendant at the parking lot where I have my clinic. I was gearing up for the morning's patients and not present at all as I drove into the lot on his first day. He beamed a gargantuan smile so warm it caught me by surprise. He waved and wished me a wonderful day with such sincerity that, despite my distracted state, I felt my body take in his good wishes and woke to the present moment. I smiled back, and the smile stayed with me into the elevator, where I was moved to share it with others heading upstairs. Day after day, Karim greeted me, and every other arrival, with a cheerful anecdote or a charitable observation or a wholehearted smile and wave. I marveled at his generosity, and I felt the power of his influence.

Karim noticed when folks drove in seeming sad or distracted or annoyed and he hoped he could lift them out of their discomfort, if only for a moment. He was intentional about making a difference: "We all know our date of entry to this life but none of us knows our exit date," he said. "So, every day I wake up it is a gift, and I want to give back." Karim's greeting became a reminder and encouragement for me each day to be present and genuinely contact others whenever I could.

PRACTICE: WHERE CAN YOU LEAD?

Whether you work in a retail or service industry, in health care or education, in a trade or a corporate environment or in a volunteer organization, you can be a leader. Can you think of situations at your workplace where you might be able to foster more safety or connection? List the ways you might show up more authentically and invite others to do the same. How could you allow yourself to matter and feel how others matter also, and how might you communicate that? For example, could you make more eye contact? Could you listen more? Might you take the time to notice how another person's undesirable reaction reflects their dysregulated unrest, and then exhale and regulate yourself so you do not react back? Can you begin to see yourself as a person influencing others by being well regulated? That is success!

Inspiring Change

Our ability to share ideas is greater than ever, yet we still struggle to engage as biological beings, feeling together in our hearts and bodies. Unrest is the shimmering entry point for the next phase of our evolution. It's time to experience our interconnectedness even as we embrace our diversity. We need to be agents of transformation for each other, creating safety to feel the heartbeat of our shared humanity. So how do we create a culture that holds us all in the truth of human vulnerability? How do we foster conditions so all of us may bow to discomfort and experience the inner riches of emotion? By embracing unrest, we grow our capacities to become an invitation to others, so they can matter also. When we have the courage to matter in our vulnerability, we can care for ourselves, each other, and the planet with the joy of being alive.

The need to face painful realities and listen and connect with each other has never been more critical. The summons to live and lead vulnerably is echoing in our culture in a new and urgent way. All over the world people are waking up to the need to face difficult truths and make radical change. We must grow our ability to engage in uncomfortable conversations, understand each other, and act. Yet in the face of these challenges, too many of us tune out, shut down, feel overwhelmed, and barrier ourselves in silos of sameness, listening to echo chambers of our own defensiveness. Why do people disengage? What is happening inside us when we numb out and disconnect from painful reality? What prompts us to look away when faced with uncomfortable information?

Many factors feed our tendency to shield ourselves, including denial, exhaustion, overwhelm, defensive shame and anger, and hopelessness. Our identity and feelings of belonging can be tied up in our beliefs. But underpinning all these reactions is unconscious avoidance of the invisible spike of unrest. We block painful reality because we unconsciously fear we cannot bear what it would feel like to face it. But if you come home to your body and matter, everything can matter. You can bear pain when you've soothed unrest because you recognize pain not as threat to life, but as a prod to live fully. So, rather than disengage, you have conversations and take actions that before seemed too hard or too painful or just pointless. Your compassion for yourself permeates every cell in your body and emanates like grace toward others and the world.

Change is overdue and imperative. The more we embrace our particular, vulnerable humanity, the more we can sense our common humanity. We are each called to give what we can to lift up those who have less. Yet as we go toward fostering all human potential, we benefit from avoiding rigid, polarizing doctrines and shaming practices. Many educators are working today to awaken us to our privilege, decolonize our unconscious habits and accepted ideologies, and challenge institutions to become equitable. Brilliant, wise teachers like Irshad Manji, Chloé Valdary, and Weeze Doran describe in a variety of ways that *how* we try to make change is at least as important as the goal itself. If we want a compassionate, respectful culture, we need to address each other with compassion and respect, even when we disagree. That is vulnerable.

The more passionately you feel about something, the harder it is to tolerate someone disagreeing with you. It takes real grit to stay open and listen to someone saying things you deeply oppose. Your best intentions for having the brave conversation will dissolve in the heat of the moment of conflict if you cannot soothe unrest.

Diversity is challenging to minds that want familiarity and things in tidy boxes, but it is a force for greater growth, more creativity, and better health. If you've grown your capacity for managing inner diversity by making room for both your impulse to avoid discomfort and your desire to approach it, you can be more open to diversity in the world around you and engage more wholeheartedly with reality's complexities.

So how do you engage? "Seek first to understand and then to be understood." Stephen Covey's words illuminate a neurobiological truth: when someone feels understood, they will be more open to receiving your message. Yet when faced with someone who disagrees with you, really being curious feels vulnerable. It is easy to feel threatened when we don't see eye to eye, especially on issues that matter deeply to us. Yet for the other person to take the vulnerable step to open their mind, you need to open yours and be curious about how they got to where they are now.

As you initiate challenging conversations for change with those whose views conflict with your values, foster safety by first soothing your own nervous system. Since there may be real obstacles to agreement or even understanding, your body will be activated with the vulnerability of wanting something you cannot 100 percent control. When you bring careful attention to your shallow breath and tense muscles, your body senses this difficulty is emotional rather than an immediate physical threat. That allows you to embody a felt sense of safety that is transmitted directly to the other person via *right-brain-to-right-brain communication*. That is a nonverbal transmission that occurs without conscious processing. The tone of your voice is warm and genuine, you make good eye contact, and you are physically engaged and open to the other person. Your assured presence helps make the other person feel safer to be present with you. Being the one who sets expectations for respect and compassion is powerful. This is the opposite of shaming tactics, which tend not to improve peoples' ability to evaluate facts or reflect on their thinking or increase motivation for change.

You do not need to give up on values you hold dear, but stay open to the humanity of the other person. Attuning to unrest, soothing it as you need to, you can be curious about the other person. Ask questions to understand how they came to their views. That prevents you from oversimplifying their view or reducing the person solely to their thinking. The space you create when you listen with warm interest and nonjudgment allows people to listen to themselves. When you listen without arguing, you create an opportunity for the other person to become aware of inner inconsistencies in their position and make room for them to be stirred by their own mixed feelings. The harder you try to convince the other person, the more they feel misunderstood, threatened, and resistant. They dig in their heels because they feel defensive. The less you force your views, the less they need to resist.

PRACTICE: ENGAGING AND INSPIRING CHANGE

Choose someone in your life whose views you disagree with and invite them into a conversation exploring those differences. Realize there will be unrest on both sides. You are both human and that admission is not a bad place to start. Your first task is to notice and soothe your unrest as soon as it spikes. Once your body registers your care and settles, you will be moved by emotion. Most likely the feeling will be anger/assertion. That is not a problem. Your assertion is meant to help you hold your ground as you look for common ground.

Your anger is for you, not for the other person. Your anger supports you on the inside, so you don't have to argue on the outside. It is for your backbone, so you are not a pushover. It is for your strong legs to take your stand. You can listen and be curious about how the other person has come to their beliefs, without agreeing with them. Feel the wave move you and trust its adaptive wisdom, as it wants to fortify you. As you feel the strength inside, you can know that what the other person is saying is not about "you" but about them... They are talking about their fears and pain. Feel the strength of your anger supporting you. As your anger begins to ebb, you can appreciate the impact of the other person's views.

As the wave of anger fades you open to the next wave, as sadness rises. Sadness helps you release the fantasy that you can change someone's mind. You let go of the illusion that if you could only find the right metaphor or argue the right way or ask the right question, then you could somehow "get" them to understand and agree with you. Until you let go of that fantasy, you cannot truly hear the other person. Your nonverbal communication conveys you're there to change their mind not to understand them, unintentionally increasing their resistance. Of course, you may want to change their mind, but as your sadness releases you from your *need* for that, you show up less agitated and more flexible.

At the end of the wave of sadness you accept your limits, and hope rises. Once you accept what you cannot do, you are free to focus on what you can; you can be a powerful person who sets expectations for how to have difficult conversations. You provide a space for the other to reflect on their views. Genuinely listening and asking questions prevents you from becoming an "object" for the other person to argue with. You deny them a projection screen to run their movie. You keep treating them as a real person and you keep showing up as a real person, curious about their position, but not agreeing with them. You lead the way by regulating unrest and setting the tone of the engagement, modeling curiosity and courage.

Your conversation may help change their mind, or your mind, or it may not, but it will give you more insight and better entry points for future conversations. But more deeply, your presence is the instrument for change. Your ability to soothe unrest, feel emotion, and stay open is music that has the potential to invite others into the dance of connection.

10

experiencing life

"This very moment is the perfect teacher."
PEMA CHÖDRÖN

RE YOU ready to live in the vulnerable flow of life, stirred by unrest and moved by emotion? Are you willing to hold your stories about yourself a bit more loosely and prize the immediacy of your felt experience? Are you open to being surprised by the richness of your inner life? Your embrace of unrest gives you a path to living vulnerably, loving wholeheartedly, and giving your gifts openhandedly to the world.

To do this you must keep in mind how in-the-moment it is to experience. This is a practice, not a cognitive process, though you need to be able to reflect as you feel so you can hold your experience. You need to appreciate how automatic it is to escape the moment when there is discomfort, so you can be mindful of your exits and know how to bring yourself back home. Your precise and focused and undivided attention is required along with patience and compassion, because this little step of tuning in to unrest is really, really hard.

Embracing unrest is a living, dynamic opening to the flow of you. It is subtle and there are many places where you can be ejected from the process. As you tune in to the sensation of unrest you will find your attention span is woefully brief and you can be distracted as fast as a chimpanzee with ADD at Disney World. Your mind wants to follow threads into the past and future and really be anywhere else but right here and right now. You have wiring in your brain from your life experiences and from your ancient heritage to keep you oriented to the outside world.

So, you need to practice embracing unrest with precision, patience, and persistence. Learn the ways your body tries to get your attention in moments of vulnerability and tune in to your body the moment it stirs. Give yourself two or three tries paying undivided attention to sensations. Look for the small sigh or release that lets you know your body feels your presence—it's like a "hello," a "thank you," a slight muscular letting go.

If your body continues to brace and you don't feel the slight melting signifying you've made that inner connection, you know there is a story or movie, a defense in operation covering how it feels when your longing meets your limits. Remember, your mind is very clever and determined to deny the painful truth of vulnerability. Your protective brain is committed to avoiding this vulnerable truth with a work-around: fix it, change it, blame yourself or the world for it, or even make you not care about it. It generates compelling scenarios, promising if only you were good enough, worthy enough, or tried hard enough, then you'd have certainty and control over the things you long for.

Your job is to block those defensive maneuvers. This is a hard line, no negotiating. Imagine erecting a thick, clear

Plexiglas wall between you and the story. You can see it and hear it. You are not ignoring it because things you ignore have too much power to control you. You acknowledge it, but you are not giving it any attention. You decide (through conscious effort) to redirect your attention back to the sensations in your body. Despite the yelling and popcorn being thrown by the fearmongering critics and bozos from behind the Plexiglas, you turn your focus to the tension in your muscles and breathe your full awareness into them, feeling slowly, carefully like nothing else in the world matters.

This dynamic process can take multiple bids before you soothe the body enough to enter the flow of emotion, and beneath that to the core of yourself. As your body lets go, in that softening you will feel some layer of truth open itself to reflection. You become aware of how you've expected something that isn't possible or denied your limits or rejected your needs or run away from pain. You will see how you have held on to a belief that you are insufficient, that there is something you need to do before you can earn your place in life, or rest and enjoy your life, or win the love you long for. And though you may have had that thought before, you are surprised at how different it is to feel it embodied with compassion. You will look at the conflict and know it to be a lie. Even though you long for things and cannot ultimately secure them, there is nothing wrong with your longing or your limits. You are enough in your vulnerable self.

You'll know when you get there because you'll sense an opening, an ease, a feeling of being enough just as you are in this moment. All the arguments with reality are quiet now. You can feel your breath in your body and the beating of your heart, and you know yourself to be part of life, flowing with your inner experience and alive to the moment. You have harnessed vulnerability to become more fully yourself. Welcome home.

Technology for Growth

The technology for transformation is at your fingertips. It is in the nerve fibers and muscles and blood of your own body. Signaled by unrest, your point of contact with vulnerability heralds your invitation to matter in the precise moment uncertainty and limits reveal you as human. That is not danger and you do not need to avoid yourself. Hear the whisperings from your body and feel the hunger from your soul and come home. Your main challenge is no longer avoiding immediate physical danger but approaching the tenderness of your heart, where your wants and desires bump up against fundamental human limits. The longing to experience your life is a beacon from your depths, illuminating your path toward feeling everything and becoming all you are meant to be.

There has never been a more important time for us to fathom our relationship with vulnerability. We live in remarkably challenging times. As a twenty-first-century human, you face fewer immediate threats to life than humans who came before, yet more emotional ones. Massive uncertainties abound in accelerating climate change; relentless social media pressure; pandemic outbreaks; the escalation of totalitarianism; the rise of surveillance capitalism; and the advent of powerful, uncontrolled new technologies. In the face of these large threats, you may become paralyzed with anxiety and despair if you do not yield to the inner experience of unrest and soothe your body. Your vulnerability is your strength, and it will grow you. You *can* do the opposite of what comes naturally. Unrest spikes and heralds your arrival on the cusp of an unfolding phenomenon of being. Waves of emotion rise like chariots to carry you to deeper levels of yourself, helping you access and expand your gifts and capacities. That moment is no longer to be feared and avoided.

It is now your friend, and with each brave approach into your experience, your human tension needle comes to balance where your soul's hunger to experience is fulfilled, even as your body's need to keep you alive is honored.

To live, to love, to care is vulnerable. You long for things and you cannot ultimately secure them. Impermanence makes every evanescent moment shimmer. And all this tenderness is what makes your human experience so radiant and meaningful and transformative. Lean toward yourself in your vulnerability and experience the joy of reunion as your body welcomes you home and your soul is liberated to feel life. You are always but a moment, a half breath, away from the loving light of your awareness meant to soothe your body. Embrace unrest, harness vulnerability, and spark growth.

acknowledgments

WANT TO acknowledge my great good fortune, in 2008, to have attended an SFU writers' workshop with editor and publishing consultant Scott Steedman, who saw potential when this book was percolating. His kind encouragement and superb guidance inspired me to bring my own vulnerable experience and whole heart to this project, or as he said, "have skin in the game." Scott also connected me with the wonderful team at Page Two. I am grateful for the calm clarity of principal Jesse Finkelstein's vision, the openhearted wisdom of editor Kendra Ward, and the skill and enthusiasm of the entire team. I stand in awe of the magical alchemy of Caitlin Fitzpatrick and Casey Carroll at Bold Woman Brands, who transformed my passionate, universe-sized ideas into clear core values so I can share my message without talking peoples' ears off.

I am blessed to have been mentored by some wise and gifted people. Early in my career I was exposed to Dr. Gordon Neufeld's beautiful work on adaptation through his Neufeld Institute Intensive One. His embrace of sadness as a path to maturation by accepting reality transformed my clinical work. I feel deeply indebted to Jon Frederickson, who is a mentor to me. His unflinching courage to lean toward pain and gently coax it out of hiding so people can heal, his precision as he tracks the living moment with his patients, and his lucid precision in formulating clinical interventions have fostered my professional growth and have been lessons for living.

A heartfelt thank you to all my dear friends who have kindly read parts of the book and said helpful and supportive things and never looked at me like I was nuts to spend weekends and holidays working on this project for so many years. You know who you are. I especially thank my dear friend Denise Buote, whose organizational genius and creative problem-solving rescued me again and again. Denise, you are closer than family and more precious to me than you know.

I gratefully acknowledge the extraordinary debt I owe to the brave people who have opened their vulnerable hearts to me, hoping to free themselves from the prison of unconscious habits to avoid their truth. Your journeys have transformed me.

And finally, I want to thank my husband, Kelly Farnsworth, whose first words to me were a stuttered, "You're so dy-dynamic." In the dy-dynamic unfolding of our shared life, your own tender vulnerability, unyielding faith, and abiding love invite me to come home to each vulnerable moment and make me want to experience everything.

selected bibliography

T HIS BIBLIOGRAPHY is a small window into some of the research and writings that have influenced my journey to understand vulnerability, emotion, anxiety, and our human longing for growth. I have chosen some of my favorite writings on developmental psychology, neurobiology, psychodynamic therapy, experiential processes, and mindfulness practices.

Books

Abbass, Allan. *Reaching Through Resistance: Advanced Psychotherapy Techniques*. Kansas City: Seven Leaves Press, 2015.

Bastian, Brock. *The Other Side of Happiness: Embracing a More Fearless Approach to Living*. London: Allen Lane, 2019.

Beck, Martha. *The Way of Integrity: Finding the Path to Your True Self*. New York: The Open Life/A Penguin Life Book, 2021.

Bolte Taylor, Jill. *Whole Brain Living: The Anatomy of Choice and the Four Characters That Drive Our Life*. Carlsbad, CA: Hay House, 2021.

Brach, Tara. *Radical Compassion: Learning to Love Yourself and Your World with the Practice of RAIN.* New York: Viking Life, 2019.

Brown, Brené. *Daring Greatly: How the Courage to be Vulnerable Transforms the Way We Live.* New York: Gotham, 2011.

———. *Dare to Lead: Brave Work. Whole Hearts. Tough Conversations.* New York: Random House, 2018.

Burkeman, Oliver. *The Antidote: Happiness for People Who Can't Stand Positive Thinking.* New York: Allen Lane, 2012.

Chödrön, Pema. *When Things Fall Apart: Heart Advice for Difficult Times.* Boulder: Shambala, 1997.

Covey, Stephen. *The Seven Habits of Highly Effective People*, 30th anniversary edition. New York: Simon and Schuster, 2020.

Damasio, Antonio. *The Feeling of What Happens: Body and Emotion in the Making of Consciousness.* Boston: Mariner Books, 2000.

Davanloo, Habib. *Basic Principles and Technique in Short-Term Dynamic Psychotherapy.* New York: Spectrum Publications, 1978.

———. *Intensive Short-Term Dynamic Psychotherapy: Selected Papers of Habib Davanloo.* New York: Wiley, 2001.

———. *Unlocking the Unconscious: Selected Papers of Habib Davanloo, MD.* Chichester, UK: Wiley, 1990.

Doidge, Norman. *The Brain That Changes Itself: Stories of Personal Triumph from the Frontiers of Brain Science.* New York: Penguin, 2007.

Fosha, Diana. *The Transforming Power of Affect: A Model for Accelerated Change.* New York: Basic Books, 2000.

Frederickson, Jon. *Co-creating Change: Effective Dynamic Therapy Techniques.* Kansas City: Seven Leaves Press, 2013.

———. *The Lies We Tell Ourselves: How to Face the Truth, Accept Yourself, and Create a Better Life.* Kansas City: Seven Leaves Press, 2017.

Hanson, Rick. *Hardwiring Happiness: The New Brain Science of Contentment, Calm, and Confidence.* New York: Harmony, 2016.

Hardy, Benjamin. *Willpower Doesn't Work: Discover the Hidden Keys to Success.* New York: Hachette, 2018.

Johnson, Sue. *Hold Me Tight: Seven Conversations for a Lifetime of Love.* New York: Hachette, 2008.

Keltner, Dacher. *Born to Be Good: The Science of a Meaningful Life.* New York: W.W. Norton & Company, Inc. 2009.

LeDoux, Joseph. *The Emotional Brain: The Mysterious Underpinnings of Emotional Life.* New York: Simon and Schuster, 1996.

Lewis, Thomas, Fara Amini, and Richard Lannon. *A General Theory of Love.* New York: Vintage, 2001.

Manji, Irshad. *Don't Label Me: An Incredible Conversation for Divided Times*. New York: St. Martin's Press, 2019.

Maté, Gabor. *When the Body Says No: The Cost of Hidden Stress*. Toronto: Vintage Canada, 2004.

Neff, Kristen. *Fierce Self-Compassion: How Women Can Harness Kindness to Speak Up, Claim Their Power, and Thrive*. New York: Harper Wave, 2021.

Neufeld, Gordon, and Gabor Maté. *Hold On to Your Kids: Why Parents Matter*. Toronto: Knopf Canada, 2004.

O'Donohue, John. *Anam Cara: A Book of Celtic Wisdom*. New York: Harper Perennial, 1998.

Pert, Candace. *Molecules of Emotion: The Science Behind Mind-Body Medicine*. New York: Scribner, 1999.

Rogers, Fred. *The World According to Mr. Rogers: Important Things to Remember*. New York: Hachette, 2019.

Samuel, Julia. *This Too Shall Pass: Stories of Change, Crisis, and Hopeful Beginnings*. Toronto: Penguin Random House of Canada, 2021.

Schore, Allan. *Right Brain Psychotherapy*. New York: W.W. Norton & Company, Ltd., 2019.

Siegel, Daniel. *Pocket Guide to Interpersonal Neurobiology: An Integrated Handbook of the Mind*. New York: W.W. Norton & Company, Ltd., 2012

Simmons, Phillip. *Learning to Fall: The Blessings of an Imperfect Life*. New York: Bantam Books, 2000.

Tronick, Ed. *The Neurobehavioral and Social-Emotional Development of Infants and Children*. New York: W.W. Norton & Company, Ltd., 2007.

Warshow, Susan Warren. *A Therapist's Handbook to Dissolve Shame and Defense: Master the Moment*. New York: Routledge, 2022.

Articles

Burns, John. W., Phillip Quartana, and Stephen Bruehl. "Anger Suppression and Subsequent Behaviors among Chronic Low Back Pain Patients: Moderating Effects of Anger Regulation Style." *Annals of Behavioral Medicine* 42, no. 1 (August 2011): 42–54.

Damasio, A.R. "The Somatic Marker Hypothesis and the Possible Functions of the Prefrontal Cortex." *Philosophical Transactions of the Royal*

Society of London Biological Sciences 351, no. 1346 (October 29, 1996): 1413-20.

Fagundes, Christopher, Ryan L. Brown, Michelle A. Chen, Kyle W. Murdock, Levi Saucedo, Angie LeRoy, E. Lydia Wu, Luz M. Garcini, et al. "Grief, Depressive Symptoms, and Inflammation in the Spousally Bereaved." *Psychoneuroendocrinology* 100 (October 2018): 190-97.

Farb, Norman, and Wolf E. Mehling. "Editorial: Interoception, Contemplative Practice and Health." *Frontiers in Psychology* 7 (December 2016).

Hojat, M., S. Mangione, T.J. Nasca, S. Rattner, J.B. Erdmann, J.S. Gonnella, M. Magee. "An Empirical Study of Decline in Empathy in Medical School." *Medical Education* 38, no. 9 (September 2004): 934-41.

Hong, M., W.H. Lee, J.H. Park, T.Y. Yoon, D.S. Moon, S.M. Lee, G.H. Bahn. "Changes of Empathy in Medical College and Medical School Students: 1-Year Follow Up Study." *BMC Medical Education* 12, no. 122 (2012): doi.org/10.1186/1472-6920-12-122.

House, J.S., K.R. Landis, and D. Umberson. "Social Relationships and Health." *Science* 241, no. 4865 (July 1988): 540-45.

Houston, Otis. "Back Into the Fold: An Interview with Chloe Valdary." *Los Angeles Review of Books*, December 12, 2019. lareviewofbooks. org/article/back-into-the-fold-an-interview-with-chloe-valdary/.

Hur, Juyoen, Jason F. Smith, Kathryn A. DeYoung, Allegra S. Anderson, Jinyi Kuang, Hyung Cho Kim, Rachael M. Tillman, Manuel Kuhn, Andrew S. Fox, and Alexander Shackman. "Anxiety and the Neurobiology of Temporally Uncertain Threat Anticipation." *The Journal of Neuroscience* 40, no. 41 (2020): 7949-64.

Lyons-Ruth, Karlen, Nadia Bruschweiler-Stern, Alexandra M. Harrison, Alexander C. Morgan, Jeremy P. Nahum, Louis Sander, Daniel N. Stern, and Edward Z. Tronick. "Implicit Relational Knowing: Its Role in Development and Psychoanalytic Treatment." *Infant Mental Health Journal* 19, no. 3 (1998): 282-89.

Murphy, Sean, and Brock Bastian. "Emotionally Extreme Life Experiences Are More Meaningful." *The Journal of Positive Psychology* 15, no. 11 (July 2019): 1-12.

Novaes, Morgana M., Fernanda Palhano-Fontes, Heloisa Onias, Katia Andrade, Bruno Loao-Soares, Tiago Arruda-Sanchez, Elisa H. Kozasa, Danilo F. Santaella, and Draulio Barros de Araujo. "The Effects of Yoga Respiratory Practice (Bhastrika Pranayama) on Anxiety, Affect, and Brain Functional Connectivity: A Randomized

Control Trial." *Frontiers in Psychiatry* (May 2020): doi.org/10.3389/
fpsyt.2020.00467.

Pohontsch, N.J., A. Stark, M. Ehrhardt, T. Kötter, and M. Scherer.
"Influences on Students' Empathy in Medical Education:
An Exploratory Interview Study with Medical Students in Their
Third and Last Year." *BMC Medical Education* 18, no. 231 (2018):
doi.org/10.1186/s12909-018-1335-7.

ten Have-de Labije, Josette. "When Patients Enter with Anxiety on the
Forefront." *Ad Hoc Bulletin of Short-Term Dynamic Psychotherapy* 10,
no. 2 (April 2006): 35–69.

Umberson, Debra, and Jennifer Karas Montez. "Social Relationships
and Health: A Flashpoint for Health Policy." *Journal of Health and
Social Behavior* (2010): 51.

Podcasts and Videos

According to Weeze. Podcast with Louise Doran, accordingtoweeze.com/.

"BC Health Officer Fights Back Tears Amid Latest COVID-19
Infections." BC, CBC News. Accessed October 8, 2021. Video, 2:11.
cbc.ca/player/play/1708090435753.

"Still Face Experiment Dr. Edward Tronick." UMass Boston. November
30, 2009. Video, 2:48. youtube.com/watch?v=apzXGEbZht0.

"TEDxPortsmouth—Dr. Alan Watkins—Being Brilliant Every Single Day
(Part 1)." TEDx Talks. March 13, 2012. Video, 18:41. youtube.com/
watch?v=q06YIWCR2Js.

Weil, Andrew. "Video: Breathing Exercises: 4-7-8 Breath." Video, 3:18.
drweil.com/videos-features/videos/breathing-exercises-
4-7-8-breath/.

Movies

Docter, Pete, dir. *Soul*. Disney/Pixar, 2020.

Flemming, Victor, dir. *The Wizard of Oz*. Beverly Hills:
Metro-Goldwyn-Mayer, 1939.

Weir, Peter, dir. *Fearless*. Burbank: Warner Bros., 1993.

index

about the author

SANDRA PARKER, PhD, is a registered psychologist who, over the past thirty years, has helped people turn toward their inner experience with compassion. She invites people to understand unrest as a call to come home to the body in moments of vulnerability, to resolve anxiety, depression, and loss of intimacy. Her practice explores ideas from developmental psychology, neurobiology, psychodynamic therapy, experiential processes, and mindfulness practices.

In addition to loving her work, she spends joyful time with her hands in the earth gardening, hiking in the woods, bicycling around the city, and can (not often enough) be found curled up on a sofa with a stiff cup of tea and a good book.

She earned her doctoral degree at the University of British Columbia, in Vancouver, and is a member of the BC Psychological Association, Canadian Psychological Association, and Canadian Register of Health Service Providers in Psychology.

Sandra lives by the ocean in beautiful Vancouver, British Columbia, with her husband and three feisty little dogs, who teach her daily about risking feeling everything.

drsandraparker.com

Made in the USA
Las Vegas, NV
14 April 2023

70593821R00159